THE NATIONAL PLATFORM OF COMMON SENSE

BY

T. J. O'HARA

TELEMACHUS PRESS

If you purchased this book without a cover you should be aware that this book is stolen property. It was reported as "unsold and destroyed" to the publisher and neither the author nor the publisher has received any payment for this "stripped book."

This book is a work of satire. As such it is meant as a humorous yet thought-provoking presentation of the National Platform of Common Sense. Except as noted, the opinions expressed within this book are solely those of the author.

THE NATIONAL PLATFORM OF COMMON SENSE
Copyright © 2010 by T. J. O'Hara. All rights reserved, including the right to reproduce this book, or portions thereof, in any form. No part of this text may be reproduced, transmitted, downloaded, decompiled, reverse engineered, or stored in or introduced into any information storage and retrieval system, in any form or by any means, whether electronic or mechanical without the express written permission of the author. The scanning, uploading, and distribution of this book via the internet or via any other means without the permission of the publisher is illegal and punishable by law. Please purchase only authorized electronic editions, and do not participate in or encourage electronic piracy of copyrighted materials.
Depend ® is a registered trademark of Kimberly Clark Worldwide, Inc.

The publisher does not have any control over and does not assume any responsibility for author or third-party websites or their content.

Cover Art Design: Lorraine Hansen
Cover Photography: Kimberly O'Hara
Cover Art Illustrations:
    Copyright © istockphoto/Bob Ash (8115166)
    Copyright © istockphoto/adroach (5840250)

Interior Art Illustrations:
    Copyright © istockphoto/Mr_Vector (2366458)

Visit The Common Sense Czar's website at
http://www.TheCommonSenseCzar.net

Become a "Follower" of The CommonSense Czar's blog at
http://TheCommonSenseCzar.blogspot.com

ISBN: 978-1-935670-32-2 (eBook)
ISBN: 978-1-935670-33-9 (Paperback)

Published by: Telemachus Press, LLC
http://www.telemachuspress.com

Printed in the United States of America

10 9 8 7 6 5 4 3 2 1

THE NATIONAL PLATFORM
OF
COMMON SENSE

T. J. O'HARA

DEDICATION

To my beautiful bride, Kimberly, who inspires and supports me in everything I do ... and to the rest of *"the Pack,"* Nikki, London and Chanel, who lay by my side as I write and bring me their toys when they think I need a break.

FOREWORD

In the interest of full disclosure ... or should I say "*complete transparency?*" ... I am the product of a *mixed marriage:* my father was a Republican, and my mother was a Democrat. To add to the complexity: my father was of Irish heritage, and my mother was of Italian heritage; my father was Catholic, and my mother was Protestant; and, my father was a male, and my mother was a female (... I think you have to *specify* that these days).

My father grew up on an Irish-only street. By that I mean, as the son of an Irish immigrant, he was safe ... on *his* street. However, he could not walk through the street that stood only a block away, because *that* was a German street, and he would likely be attacked. In case you haven't seen the movie *The Streets of New York*, suffice it to say that the Irish held a unique status at the time that was somewhere between that of the early colonial slaves ... and pond scum.

My mother was the first-born child of Italian immigrants. Back in those days, Italians enjoyed a higher status that the Irish (... but then, who didn't?) until that nettlesome thing called World War II broke out. Italy, you see, was part of the *Axis of Power* along with Germany and Japan; bad news for Italian descendants living in the United States. Never mind that my grandparents were more proud of their United States citizenship than anyone you can imagine or that my mother never set foot in Italy; they were singled out during WWII, and their home was painted by the apparent progeny of today's *"taggers"* with a less-than-artistic swastika.

To add to the confusion, my father was a blue-collar worker, who worked for the newspaper as a journeyman and served as his union's Secretary/Treasurer. In that latter capacity, my sister and I earned part of our meager allowances by helping him balance the books and write the monthly union report. When technology displaced the need for his craft, my father's union lost its battle with a competing union for jurisdiction. As a result, he became an entrepreneur and started a modest but successful house painting business. He had bravely served as a commando in the Navy during WWII, often hitting the beaches in the South Pacific with the first wave of Marines. It was an experience in his life that he generally chose not to discuss. But I have no doubt, were he alive today and this country's freedom at stake, he would take up arms once again without a moment's hesitation ... for he loved this country that much.

Let me apologize ahead of time for the *"political incorrectness"* of the next statement, but it's the truth: my mother was a *"stay-at-home-mom."* There, I said it! Boy, it was sure hard to get it out, but I feel quite relieved.

My mother was always there for my sister and me when we came home from school; she cared for us when we were ill and was active in anything that she thought might contribute in a meaningful way to our lives (*e.g.,* PTA, Playground Mother's Club, etc.). She was passionate about art and music and made sure that we had an appreciation for both. And Mom was in the audience anytime we spoke, sang, acted or played. She also was a member of the local Civic Association, which was as close as she came to political activism. Yet, she was deeply steeped in the national pride that is so often associated with America's *Greatest Generation* and was further driven by one of her parents' favorite phrases: *"God bless America!"*

So now you know! I take my citizenship *very* seriously. While I was *born* into it and didn't have to traverse an ocean or learn a new language, as both sets of my grandparents did, I have a *profound* respect for what it means. Neither did I have to survive the economic hardships of *The Great Depression* nor defend my country on foreign soil as my parents did. However, perhaps it is through the intensity of my family members' experiences and their devotion to what this Nation stands for that has given birth to my undying *love* for ... and *commitment* to ... the United States of America.

And as far as *"political correctness"* goes ... if that concept is meaningful to you, you may wish to read no further because I have no time for such folly. I was raised to *"tell the truth, the whole truth, and nothing but the truth ... so help me God."* If unvarnished honesty offends you, read no further. If the fact that I choose to occasionally call upon the *"help"* of a higher power offends you, read no further. However, if you can muster the strength to weather those two concepts, I encourage you to read on.

I write *not* to *convince* you ... but rather to *entertain* you and to *stimulate your thoughts* so that your opinion, moving forward, is more *informed* and reflects *your* true feelings rather than what *someone else* would have you believe. Brace yourself ... and enjoy the journey!

THE NATIONAL PLATFORM
OF
COMMMON SENSE

INTRODUCTION

*** If you've already read the Introduction in one of the other books you may skip this chapter ***

By way of introduction, I am the self-appointed *Common Sense Czar*. With all due respect to Thomas Paine, author of *Common Sense*, I think I deserve the job. Besides, Thomas Paine has been dead for over 200 years ... even though he's still registered to vote in three States according to Acorn.

Being a Czar is really cool. Unlike politicians, you don't have to have to raise money to run; you generally don't have to be vetted in a rigorous way; and you have reasonably unbridled authority ... *plus*, you get to be called *"Czar!"*

As the *Common Sense Czar*, I apply *common sense* to the issues of the day; something that has been missing in our Nation's capital for quite some time. As my first official act, I applied *common sense* to the current glut of Czars and dismissed all of them except for the *Faith-Based Czar*. Personally, I can't imagine why the ACLU hasn't attacked that particular position with its normal zeal. The *issue* would seem to be *obvious*. Maybe it's *Devine intervention*. If that's the case, my *common sense* tells me not to *mess* with it.

As for the rest of the positions, the decisions were easy. The *Guantanamo Closure Czar* was going to lose his job anyway since his position was driven by an Executive Order issued by President Obama on January 22, 2009, to close Gitmo *"no later than one year from now"* to quote the President, and we all know how well that's been going.

The *TARP Czar* and *Stimulus Accountability Czar* were also expendable. On February 25, 2009, just eight days after signing the $787-billion dollar economic stimulus package, President Obama stated that he was putting Vice President Joe Biden in charge of the *"tough, unprecedented oversight effort"* of the fiscal stimulus plan *"because nobody messes with Joe."* I can't imagine why we would need these two Czars if Vice President Biden has everything under control.

The departure of the *Government Performance Czar* was another easy call given our Government's performance in recent years.

I dumped the *Afghanistan Czar* and the *Sudan Czar* because, the last time I looked, these are independent countries. If we have military or humanitarian initiatives in *any* country, it's Congress' responsibility to address the issues. We don't need Czars for specific countries. If we did, then we should at least start with Russia. They're used to it.

Then, we've got the *Mideast Peace Czar*. Talk about a dead-end job! These countries have been fighting for over 2,000 years. What are the odds that a political appointee in the United States will be able to resolve their differences? That's one more position we can eliminate. And while we're at it, let's eliminate the *Central Region Czar* who is responsible for our policies in, you guessed it, the same part of the world; needless duplication. Gone!

While we're on the subject, we presently have a *Terrorist Czar*. No, not Bill Ayres (although he might be a good choice under the assumption that *"it takes one to know one"*) ... a fellow named John Brennan. This is the same John Brennan who allegedly nixed a plan to kill or capture Osama bin Laden back in 1998. Way to establish job security! Eliminating this position shouldn't exactly create a void.

Staying with the terrorist theme for a moment, I see we have a *Weapons Czar* and a *WMD Policy Czar*. Why differentiate? If the *Weapons Czar* only tackles issues of conventional weaponry (like sling-shots), we don't need him. If there really are *"no weapons of mass destruction,"* we don't need the *WMD Policy Czar* either. Assuming for the moment that weapons of mass destruction are *not* just a figment of former President Bush's imagination, I'll establish the policy. Weapons of mass destruction are bad things; particularly in the hands of unstable people. There you have it ... a *common sense* policy and two more positions eliminated.

Along these same lines, we have an *Intelligence Czar*. Let's just agree that it's an obvious oxymoron and eliminate the position to stop the snickering!

We have a *Border Czar* to protect us from illegal immigration. If you call this Czar's office, press 1 for English, press 2 for Spanish, press 3 for Tagalog, press 4 for Farsi, press 5 for ... well, you get the picture. Applying *common sense*: we have immigration laws in place. Enforce them! One more position eliminated.

This same solution can be applied to two more positions: *Domestic Violence Czar* and *Drug Czar*. *Common sense* tells us that domestic violence and the illegal use of drugs are bad. We have laws in place against both negative behaviors. Enforce them! That gets rid of those two Czars.

Next, we have a few positions tied to specific locations within our country. We have a *Great Lakes Czar*. I've been to the Lakes. They're indeed *"Great."* That should cover it. Position eliminated!

We also have a *California Water Czar* ... as if there aren't any other problems in that State. Interestingly enough, this particular one is man-made. Last year, California and the surrounding States enjoyed record snowfalls, which created an abundance of water. However in 2007, a Federal judge ruled that endangered smelt might get caught in the pumps. So, the pumps were ordered to be shut down to preserve the habitat for the tiny, silver fish. As a result, taxpayers from San Diego to San Jose have been placed on water allocation and have suffered significant rate hikes; farmers have been threatened with foreclosures and bankruptcies because they can't irrigate their crops; but I'm happy to say that the smelt are enjoying living their lives and being eaten by natural predators. I apologize in advance to environmentalists, but there comes a time when *common sense* must intervene. So, I say open the pumps, restore the agrarian economy, fish fry at my house, and eliminate this position.

Since I've already offended my fellow environmentalists, let's take a look at three other unnecessary positions: *Climate Czar, Energy and Environment Czar*, and *Green Jobs Czar*. If we accept the premise of Global Warming (as established by world-renowned scientist and inventor of the Internet, Al Gore), our climate would seem to be a legitimate issue. Luckily, the Federal and State governments have authority to create laws that make us better *"citizens of the planet."* Unfortunately, we have no authority to legislate what China, India and the rest of the world do. So, the *Climate Czar* can step down.

Similarly, we don't have a need for an *Energy and Environment Czar*. The environmental element is repetitive and, as for energy, I can set the policy: eliminate our dependence on foreign oil; cultivate our natural resources in a responsible way (which doesn't mean *"rape the earth"* any more than it means that accessing them will destroy the world as we know it); and develop new and better alternative fuels.

This brings us to the *Green Job Czar*, but I need not address this one. Apparently, the White House has already excused him when it was discovered that he took the whole Czar thing a little too literally and pledged allegiance to Stalin. Besides, the title evokes a theme of racial discrimination.

Speaking of jobs, I find it interesting that we don't have a *Jobs Czar*. No problem ... I can handle it. We do have an *Economic Czar*, so maybe there's some overlap. Paul Volcker headed the Federal Reserve during the latter stages of the Carter Administration and through the Reagan years. The good news is that he is credited with helping our Nation overcome *"stagflation."* The bad news is that he did it by raising the prime lending rate to 21.5% and driving the economy into a deep recession that created a level of unemployment not seen since the Great Depression. I'm eliminating his position because we're already there when it comes to creating a recession and experiencing an untenable level of unemployment.

Correspondingly, I'm going to eliminate the *Regulatory Czar*. I've soured on the self-righteousness of our regulatory agencies ever since the *"anointed one,"* Eliot Spitzer, prostituted his position as Governor of New York after ruling herd over the bastions of Wall Street. I'll only reconsider if Bernie Madoff gets an early parole and assumes the role of Frank Abagnale, Jr. (I hope that reference isn't too esoteric). Besides, the current *Regulatory Czar* apparently wants to *"regulate"* everything including *"free speech"* (of which I am obviously a fan); having called for taxing or censoring conspiracy theories ... such as the theory that Global Warming may be a deliberate fraud. He also wants to lobby for the right for animals to bring lawsuits. This would give even more power to the ACLU (America's Crazy Lunatic Unit) to bring "udderly" worthless lawsuits on behalf of sacred cows; barring them from grazing on government property as a violation of the separation of church and state. Gone!

We also have a *Pay Czar*. This is the individual who, like the *Regulatory Czar*, remains ever vigilant over those fat-cat CEOs in high-profile industries we all love to hate. However, I can't help noticing that he hasn't imposed any restrictions on the compensation of the executives at Fannie Mae and Freddie Mac, who have almost single-handedly destroyed the economy. I also don't recall seeing any *"smack downs"* of the union officials who can consistently deliver political votes in volume. *Common sense* tells me he has to go!

While we're talking about unions, I feel compelled to point out that we have two Czars for the automotive industry: a *Car Czar* and an *Auto Recovery Czar*. By now, you know how I feel about redundancy. I'm not sure what either does, but I'm *sure* we don't need two. Under the *Car Czar's* guidance, both General Motors and Chrysler have gone bankrupt. Since I'm reasonably confident they could have accomplished that without him, his position is being eliminated. As for the *Auto Recovery Czar*, I'm not sure if he's vested with the responsibility to help the automotive industry *"recover"* from the bankruptcies the *Car Czar* has overseen, or if his responsibility is to *"recover"* the taxpayer dollars that have been funneled into the industry without any noticeable results. Once again, this is a position we can safely eliminate.

Moving along into the vital science, technology and information sectors, I am happy to say we have a Czar for each one. Our *Science Czar* is a top-flight academic, which means that *common sense* isn't a part of his world. He once proffered the idea of forced abortions, *"compulsory sterilization,"* and the creation of a *"Planetary Regime"* to control human population and natural resources to save the Earth. *"Earth to Science Czar,"* I'll only consider keeping you if the *"compulsory sterilization"* idea begins with Members of our current Congress.

Our *Technology Czar* and *Information Czar* are good friends. Together, they will lead the evolution of Information Technology within our government. You guessed it ... I see this as redundant. Given that the *Information Czar* came first and brought the *Technology Czar* on board, I've got to give the nod to him. Unfortunately, he's been linked to hiring individuals with criminal records to protect our information. Since I'd hate to break up a team, they both have to go.

With healthcare reform on the forefront, we have two Czars that touch upon it: an *AIDS Czar* and a *Health Czar*. The *AIDS Czar* can go. AIDS is a disease. Other than its associated political capital, it does not rank in the top ten causes of death in the United States (which are: (1) Heart Disease; (2) Cancer; (3) Stroke; (4) Chronic Lower Respiratory Diseases; (5) Accidents (unintentional injuries); (6) Diabetes; (7) Alzheimer's disease; (8) Influenza and Pneumonia; (9) Nephritis, Nephrotic Syndrome, and Nephrosis; and (10) Septicemia). Sorry, but until the Top Ten have their own Czars, AIDS doesn't merit one. Because the *Health Czar* hasn't had the *common sense* to recognize this either, she's gone too!

I'm sad to report that we have a comparatively unaccomplished *Urban Affairs Czar*. Why settle? This is America. We have John Edwards, Bill Clinton, Mark Sanford and, most recently, Tiger Woods. Now, *these* men clearly know how to have urban affairs! If none of them will step up to embrace their civic duty, let's just eliminate this position.

So, with that task completed, let's get to work!

WHAT YOU NEED TO KNOW BEFORE YOU START

In an effort to provide a historical basis for <u>The National Platform of Common Sense</u>, the *Common Sense Czar* has incorporated a historical overview of the *Declaration of Independence*, the *Constitution*, and the *Bill of Rights* (and a few other salient Amendments) as well as his own *"politically incorrect"* commentary.

 **The *"planks"* of the *Common Sense Czar's* satirical Platform start with the *Common Sense Czar's* very own *"idea"* light bulb. They are further distinguished by their indentation and bolded text (with this section serving as an example).**

While meant to entertain, the *Common Sense Czar's* Platform positions are also meant to stimulate thought. Don't be surprised if you find yourself scratching your head and thinking, *"Hey, some of these ideas sound better than what the major political Parties are promoting."* You see ... *"common sense"* can have that kind of effect on you.

When the indentation and bolded text end, the Common Sense Czar's Platform position also ends and you are returned to his running commentary.

AN ASSESSMENT OF THE POLITICAL LANDSCAPE

This book does not reflect the beliefs of *any* particular Party. Rather it reflects the *reality-based* Platform of the Common Sense Czar (me). I distinguish it with the term *"reality-based"* because I believe that element is lacking in *either* of the mainstream Parties' Platforms that have been properly *roasted* in the other two books that comprise this trilogy.

The Democratic Platform is filled with great promise and hope as in: let's just promise *everything* to *everybody* to get elected … and then, let's *hope* there is *some* way to pay for it. Reality-based? I think not!

It also loses serious points for promoting an emotional environment that can best be described as an attempt to create The <u>Divided</u> States of America. It uses stereotypes to foster a sense of oppression and a *"We vs. They"* mentality for the singular purpose of positioning the Democratic Party as the *"knight on the white horse that can save the day."* Of course, in a Democratic fairy tale, the horse wouldn't be allowed to be white because that just wouldn't be *"politically correct."* Perhaps an American Paint would be a more appropriate choice of horse given its natural diversity of color.

This may seem to be a trivial point, but the Democrats have a strategic and tactical dependence upon *"political correctness."* Strategically, the concept is in alignment with the *"kumbaya feel"* of their Party's movement. They're all about peace, love, fairness, equality, etc. That's why their rallies are often marked by assaults, property damage, a blatant disregard for the law, and the trampling of the rights of others who are not so *"enlightened."*

From a *tactical* perspective, the Democrats use *"political correctness"* to control the Republican Party. Republicans, by and large, want to be liked. They envy the way the *"huddled masses"* seem to be attracted to the Democratic Party. They wish that *they* possessed that skill. But alas, they have been *dramatically* out-marketed by the Democrats. So, whenever the Republicans attempt to assert a difference of opinion, the Democrats smack them down with *"political correctness."* Whether it's playing the *"race card,"* claiming that Republicans are *"homophobic,"* or labeling them as some stone-age version of *"born-again Christians,"* the Democrats know how to throw a flag on the play … *"Personal foul … 15 yards and loss of down for political incorrectness"*… and the Republicans are absolutely clueless with respect to how to respond.

"Political correctness" is also tactically significant to the Democrats with respect to controlling its *own* constituencies. The challenge in orchestrating a *"divide and conquer"* strategy to build and maintain a political base (*i.e.,* splitting people into different groups within which they can more personally identify themselves based upon obvious characteristics – race, color, religion, gender, sexual orientation, etc.) resides in maintaining control across the disparate groups it creates. Enter the concept of *"political correctness." "Political correctness"* serves as a binding agent; a common cause that *"connects"* people of otherwise diverse interests. For example: a gay, Hispanic woman with one Black parent, who has a birth defect and happens to be a practicing Druid may be able to qualify for a student loan easier than you or me, but each of the *"minority"* characteristics she displays is unique from all the others. The gay community has its issues; the Hispanic community has its own; the Black community has others; those with birth defects face different challenges; and I can't tell you how hard it is to be a member of the Druid church these days! Yet, *"political correctness"* ties these groups together. It allows them to enjoy their own *individual* sense of *"oppression"* while sharing a *collective* sense of *"oppression"* with others … and this is *critical* to the Democratic Platform. Otherwise, these groups, which are *intentionally* identified in an *individual* manner by the Democratic Party, might not share any commonality at all. However, the concept of *"political correctness"* allows them to *appreciate* the pain their *"brothers and sisters"* must feel when they have been *"wronged"* … at least within the shallow context of *"political correctness!"*

The Republican Platform isn't much better. While its positions may be slightly more in alignment with reality … given that Republicans *seem* to grasp the concept of cost/benefit at least to *some* degree …the Party itself falls *well* short of being *reality-based* because it chooses to ignore the fact that it hasn't been particularly effective at leading our country when it has held majority positions in the House and Senate in recent years as well as the Oval Office. It also seems to lose touch with reality when it attempts to legislate moral absolutes that *ignore* the existence of a diversity of opinion and every individual's freedom of choice. As a result, it *routinely* paints itself into a corner from which it cannot escape.

The Republican Party is strategically and tactically *inept* from a political perspective. It has increasingly surrendered ground to the Democratic Party because it doesn't know how to communicate effectively. To use a boxing analogy, it is fighting out of its weight class. *Really good* Flyweights get knocked out by *mediocre* Heavyweights; and from a strategic and tactical basis, that is the mismatch we have in our current political system. The Republicans cannot seem to define their position in a way that is compelling to the average American and, as a result, the Democrats enjoy a healthy lead in registered voters. The Republicans' only hope is to marshal enough concern among their more limited base to drive a higher percentage of turn-out at the polls. To do that, they resort to a tactic that has already been mastered by their opponents: the establishment of *fear*. If Republicans can generate enough *fear*, they can win elections; and it is natural for people to fear the *unknown* (*i.e.*, *"Change"*). Otherwise, the numbers are not in their favor.

To stimulate *fear*, the Republicans must speak out about the type of change the Democrats seek and the cost associated therewith. *"Political correctness"* kills them on the first point to the degree that the importance of the second point is drastically reduced. For example: if the Democrats lobby for a program that panders to the special interests of a particular *"oppressed minority"* (take your pick) and the cost of such program would be significant and unjustified, the Republicans are obliged to first attack the program on its merits. This naturally *upsets* the *"oppressed minority"* to whom the program appeals. If the issue was limited to that *specific* minority, there wouldn't be a lot of risk for the Republicans; but rest assured that the Democrats are going to throw the *"politically incorrect"* flag to attract the attention of *otherwise* disinterested *"minorities."* Since the Democratic Party has mastered the ability to create a sense of community among these widely disparate groups when the *"politically incorrect"* flag is thrown, the groups respond with solidarity. Now, the Republicans have a *real* problem because the original *minority* has blossomed into a significant *majority*. If the Republicans press the issue, they will be represented to be a bunch of uncaring, selfish, stodgy, old white men with money; a sect to be reviled by any decent member of a *"minority"* ... no matter how politically *manufactured* that *"minority"* might be. As a result, the Republicans never even get to *raise* the issue of the fiscal irresponsibility of the particular program, and even if they do, no one outside of their base *listens* because their core argument has already been branded to be *"politically incorrect."* Game, set, and match to the Democrats.

Republicans also lose political momentum when they take a *"holier than thou"* approach to an issue. To placate the *extreme* Right of their constituency, they tend to *"preach"* morals; morals that they may not always honor in their *own* lives. As a result, it seems to be a far greater sin when a Republican is unfaithful to a spouse than when a Democrat has an extramarital dalliance. Thankfully, any flirtation they may have with abortion remains private. However, their stance on gay marriage sometimes is visibly at odds with their family realities. This is a political equivalent of the saying that *"when you live by the sword, you die by the sword."*

Speaking of which, as Psalm 149:6 of the Old Testament says, *"Let the high praises of God be in their mouth, and a two-edged sword in their hand."* This is another paradigm of the Republican Party. The Party has positioned itself as the *"protector"* of the people and based that protection on *National Defense* and maintaining *"Law and Order,"* which are government mandates delineated by the *Constitution*.

Interestingly enough, the Democratic Party has similarly positioned itself as the *"protector"* of the people, but they have based *their* protection on providing for the *"oppressed."* To quote Psalm 72:12-13: *"For he will deliver the needy who cry out, the afflicted who have no one to help. He will take pity on the weak and the needy and save the needy from death."* Adding to that, Psalm 74:21: *"Do not let the oppressed retreat in disgrace; may the poor and needy praise your name."* Okay, while quoting the Bible may be offensive to members of the *extreme Left*, more moderate Democrats may appreciate the irony. In any event, from a strategic perspective, following *these* scriptures seems to attract a *bigger* base. Once again, the God-fearing Republicans fail to win the day.

Whether you support them or not, you must at least feel *slightly* sorry for the Republicans. Their failure to grasp the nature of mankind has nearly rendered them *irrelevant* from a political perspective. They are *dreadfully* overmatched when they go head-to-head with the Democrats, who are much more skilled at fighting *"dirty."*

Allow me to put things in perspective before we move forward. Are you familiar with the *"Seven Deadly Sins"* ... *Pride; Avarice/Greed; Envy; Wrath/Anger; Lust; Gluttony; and Sloth?* What about the *"Opposing Virtues"*... *Humility; Generosity; Love; Kindness; Self Control; Faith/Temperance; and Zeal?* The reason I raise them is because I believe these emotional characteristics have evolved into the battle ground between the two major Parties. To wit:

- The Republicans value *Humility* while the Democrats counter by appealing to the *Pride* of each *"oppressed minority,"* and in today's world, sin trumps virtue.
  - 1 point for the Democrats
- The Democrats emphasize their *Generosity* by subtly appealing to the *Avarice* and *Greed* (*i.e.*, the special interests) of their *"oppressed minorities"* while effectively posturing the Republicans as the *Party* of *Avarice* and *Greed*.
  - 3 points for the Democrats
- The Republicans argue that the Democratic supporters *Envy* the *success* of Republican supporters while Democrats counter that they're all about *Love*.
  - 1 point for the Republicans
  - 1 point for the Democrats
- The Democrats argue that Republicans are filled with *Wrath* and *Anger* because of their strong support of *National Defense* and *"Law and Order"* while positioning themselves as the Party of *Kindness*.
  - 2 points for the Democrats
- Both sides point fingers at each other as falling prey to *Lust*, but you've got to give it to the Democrats for having refined the art; besides, can you think of any Party *other* than the Republicans when you hear the words *Self-Control?*
  - 2 points for the Republicans
- The Democrats have done a good job of emphasizing the Republicans' perceived *Gluttony* as *"fat cats,"* but the Republicans have been able to offset that sin with the virtue of *Faith* and *Temperance*; concepts which generally seem to have evaded the Democrats.
  - We'll call this round "Even"
- The Democrats' reliance on welfare relegates them to the status of *Sloth's* biggest supporter, and the Republicans' commitment to *"work ethic"* earns them the title for *Zeal*; although the *Zeal* with which the

Democrats endorse social programs and spending helps avoid a two-point loss.
- o   1.5 points for the Republicans

That's 7 points for the Democrats and 4.5 points for the Republicans ... or a ratio of 1.56:1. Let's see: the Democrats have about 86 million registered voters and the Republicans have about 55 million registered voters for a ratio of roughly 1.56:1. So, now you know! The Democrats are more skilled at exploiting our human characteristics of sin and virtue than the Republicans, which accounts for their overwhelming lead in registered voters. The Republicans rely on the fact that a sufficient percentage of their base will see through the Democratic façade and be concerned enough to go to the polls to offset the Democrats' raw numbers advantage.

As the Common Sense Czar, I believe I can create the best of both political worlds: a raw numbers advantage (as the Democrats have); and a more informed and concerned electorate (as the Republicans have). First, I'll start with the base of Independent voters who, at least on the surface, are not swayed by *either* Party's rhetoric. That puts 28 million in my camp. Then, I only need to attract about 26 percent of the registered Republicans and registered Democrats to pass *both* of them. Surely, I've got a shot at finding one *rational* voter in every four! That would make the Common Sense Party the *clear* winner in *any* national election.

Armed with that confidence, I now present to you:

The National Platform of Common Sense.

PREAMBLE

AS IT WAS IN THE BEGINNING

ONCE UPON A TIME, there lived a people who had suffered through *true* oppression. They had been governed by an elitist class (headed by one individual) that evolved through and was forever protected by blood-lines over which the people had no control. The Monarchy, as the elitist form of government came to be known, created and administered the law; defining what you could *do*, what you could *say*, how you could *worship*, and to what level you could *aspire* ... all while living in grand style. To support that grand style, as well as to maintain their control, they became adept at manipulating society through the concept of taxation. The Monarchy quickly learned that, through taxation, they could continue to suppress those who might otherwise surpass them based upon superior skills or a willingness to invest additional effort.

The Monarchy also recognized that it must quash discontent among the masses that far outnumbered the chosen few. To do this, the Monarchy *"provided"* for the masses in the form of handouts and protection. Unfortunately for the Monarchy, a small percentage of its subjects saw through the ruse and had the intestinal fortitude to do something about it. Being too small in number to overthrow the Monarchy within its own country, they chose to leave.

Now, in those days, travel was significantly more hazardous than it is today. These *"Pilgrims"* couldn't merely book a ticket over the Internet and fly to a more favorable environment. Instead, they had to huddle together in small boats that were barely sea-worthy and sail for months at a time, with little to eat or drink, to an untamed land that offered nothing more than opportunity ... an untamed land then known as America.

Through their hard work and perseverance, they began to build a new society. Never one to miss an opportunity, the Monarchy was quick to recognize that this *New World* might offer the chance to expand its empire. With the mightiest army and navy in the world, it began to make its presence known and claimed America as its own. To seal the deal, it would have to begin to impose its laws and levy taxes to, once again, gain control over the masses.

Unfortunately for the Monarchy, the Pilgrims (who were now know as Colonists) were not particularly eager to return to the state of oppression they had previously endured and suffered so much adversity to escape. So, on July 4, 1776, the Colonists issued what has come to be known as the *Declaration of Independence*.

Needless to say, the Monarchy was not particularly pleased by this turn of events and sent ships and troops to restore order. Alas, the Colonists would have none of it and chose, instead, to take on the almost insurmountable task of fighting back. Never again wanting to succumb to the control of a large and powerful government, the Colonist fought as if their lives depended upon it ... because they did. At the conclusion of a protracted Revolutionary War, the Monarchy found discretion to be the better part of valor and surrendered the *New World* to the Colonists.

Having won the Revolutionary War, our Founding Fathers were faced with a new challenge: forming a government for the *United States of America*. As a result, an extraordinary group of citizens took great care to consider the *form* of government that could best serve the people and withstand the test of time. Anarchy wasn't an option. Other than that, *"the Framers,"* as they have become known, had unbridled discretion.

They were all too familiar with Autocracies (or Dictatorships), which come in a wide variety of flavors. A dictatorship driven by bloodlines, such as the Monarchy from which they had just escaped, was clearly not a *"fit."* A Theocracy was ruled out for similar reasons. If the Framers had wanted to seize complete power, this was their chance; for in a Theocracy, the government claims to be divinely blessed and in direct contact with the God of its choosing. This even trumps a Monarchy since it allows the ruling class to enjoy an indulgent lifestyle *without* the burden of bloodlines. Thankfully, the Framers took the high road and passed on this option.

While Karl Marx (no relation to Groucho, Harpo, Chico or Zeppo) is attributed with the popularization of *modern* Communism, the core concept actually dates back to Paleolithic times, so its underpinnings were certainly up for consideration. As we view it today, Communism is based upon centralized planning by the government, which means that only *one party* and *one class* of people needs to exist. While this sounds appealing in theory, those in control of the *"one party"* inevitably view themselves as separate and superior; essentially creating yet another form of Dictatorship. Welcome to human nature at its finest! I'd like to think that the Framers *recognized* this and *intentionally* avoided heading us in that direction.

Socialism wasn't directly up for consideration because it wasn't *spawned* until the French Revolution in 1789 and more cogently described until several decades later. But for the sake of argument, let's assume that the Framers were bright enough to *"think outside the box"* and could have broadened the concept of Communism to incorporate what has evolved into Socialism. The reality is that Socialism and Communism are somewhat inbred anyway. Primitive Communism influenced Socialism, and in turn, Socialism influenced modern Communism. I believe the Framers dismissed creating this type of government for a *reason* … and remember: they had a clean slate with which to work.

Socialism, as we know it today, is offered in two flavors: Communistic and Democratic. To better understand the difference between the two, let's give a special *shout out* to Karl Marx. His *Communist Manifesto* espouses a *classless* society in which *everything* is shared and owned by *everyone*. It's the ultimate *"co-op;"* offering a majority-ruled state that basically offers *"Anarchy with a vote."* Can you say, *"Power to the people?"* It sounds *eminently* fair when you're young and impressionable, but it is fundamentally flawed in *real* life. It's hard to steer a political ship with no one at the helm, and human nature intervenes once again; leaving you with just another form of Dictatorship to *"redistribute the wealth."*

With that said, Communistic Socialism leans toward a Marxist *sharing* that is *heavily* controlled by a *single party*. Democratic Socialism is perhaps even more insidiously Marxist in that the *people* purportedly have a say and ostensibly may be represented by multiple Parties. The reality is that Democratic Socialism pits the majority against the minority and *justifies* the results with a vote. In effect, it's a form of societal genocide since the minority's position can *never* survive the vote. It is worth noting that neither of these models has *ever* worked in the real world, so they're best *left* (no pun intended) to political rallies and rock-throwing parties.

Fascism also didn't technically exist during the Framers' deliberations, but I'm reasonably certain it wouldn't have carried the day. I only bring it up because you hear the term cavalierly bandied about so often today. I though it would be good to have a clear *understanding* of what it actually means. Fascism is a blatant form of Dictatorship, but you've got to give it high marks for *transparency*. You see, Fascism just comes right out and *says* it's going to *discriminate* … for no particular reason … and in a *cruel* and *vindictive* manner. It provides a *legal* justification for separating the *"haves"* from the *"have nots"* (think Nazi Germany, which was a blend of Fascism and Socialism under the control of a Dictator – especially bad news for Catholics, Communists, the clergy, handicapped individuals, homosexuals, and those of the Jewish faith in those days). It would hardly have been worth fighting a Revolutionary War to have created a government like that.

Then, there is Democracy. *Ah, Democracy!* The most misunderstood form of government in the group. The United States is routinely describes as a Democracy. Yet, a thorough examination of the *Constitution* reveals that the word is never mentioned. Perhaps, it is because the Framers *never* intended our country to be a Democracy ... and for good reason. Democracies are predicated on *majority-rule*, which *sounds* good in theory. Resources are allocated as prescribed by the majority of the people and, theoretically, are distributed in an equitable manner. As Mr. Rogers would say, *"Can you say Socialism? Sure, you can!"* Ultimately, Democracies dissolve into Socialistic orders. While Democracies purport to limit government interference and call for multiple political parties, the *leadership* of these parties tends to evolve into a separate *class* ... apart from, but somewhat in *control* of the majority.

Another challenge with Democracies is that the majority, to the degree that it *really* votes, tends to vote in its *own* best interests ... which may not be in the long-term best interest of the *country*. In effect, it evolves into a *group* Dictatorship. For example: it sounds great to the majority to have the government provide a wide-range of services that will perceivably enhance the lives of the those who are *in* the majority and to *pay* for those services by taxing the minority. However, if the minority decides it *"no longer wants to play that game"* and decides to leave the country or abandon the characteristics that made it stand out as a minority (*i.e.*, innovative thinking, a greater willingness to take risk, a stronger work ethic, etc.), a *new* minority will have to evolve from *within* the present majority. Otherwise, who's going to pay for all this free *sh* ... uh ... *stuff?*

The Framers saw that problem coming and abandoned the idea of forming a Democracy. Sorry if that bursts your bubble! What they *did* form was a *Republican form of government* ... right there in black and white in the *Constitution* ... as it was extended to each State in Article IV, Section 4. Now, all you Democrats out there *calm down* ... and you Republicans, try not to hurt your arms patting yourselves on the back. This does *not* refer to *"Republican"* in the *"elephant"* sense (or is that *"scents?"*). It references the formation of a

Republic ... as in form of government ... as in the Pledge of Allegiance: "... *and to the Republic for which it stands."*

A Republic provides for a government driven by a *Constitution* that expresses and provides for the enforcement of the *individual* rights of its citizens (as provided for in the *Bill of Rights* and additional Amendments) and establishes the relevant branches of government and their respective authority; in our case, the *Legislative Branch* (Article I of the US Constitution), the *Executive Branch* (Article II of the US Constitution), and the *Judicial Branch* (Article III of the US Constitution). Is any of this starting to sound familiar?

Should you still think that the United States is a Democracy: when the deliberations of the Constitutional Convention of 1787 were concluded, a diary entry indicates that a certain Mrs. Powel asked Benjamin Franklin, *"Well, Doctor, what have we got, a Republic or a Monarchy?"* Without hesitation, Franklin answered, *"A Republic, if you can keep it."* History is replete with similar confirmations (as well as the denouncement of Democracies) from the mouths and/or pens of George Washington, James Madison, Alexander Hamilton, Samuel Adams, *et al*. A Republic (rather than a Democracy) is clearly what the Framers had in mind.

IT IS NOW AND EVER SHALL BE

The reason I proffered this brief history is to reinforce the mindset of those who drafted *The Constitution of the United States* and its ten companion Amendments (known as the *Bill of Rights*.) While the language of the *Constitution* and *Bill of Rights* may appear to be a bit arcane due to the beating our literacy has taken over the years, its still provides a magnificent socio-political road map to follow.

If you haven't *"visited"* these documents in recent years (or *ever*), I recommend them to your attention. The intellectual journey is inspiring and logically designed.
- The Preamble explains the purpose of the *Constitution.*
- Article I establishes the Legislative Branch (House of Representatives and the Senate).
- Article II establishes the Executive Branch (with the President serving as its Chief Executive).
- Article III establishes the Judicial Branch (a system of courts and judges).

- Article IV establishes the relationship between the Federal government and the States.
- Article V establishes how to amend the *Constitution*.
- Article VI establishes the *Constitution* as the supreme law of the land, and
- Article VII establishes the requirements for ratification of the *Constitution*.

To speed things up, I shall review the first three Articles and the *Bill of Rights* (and other salient Amendments) as I unfold the *National Platform of Common Sense*. Suffice it to say that the *Constitution* and its Amendments are as important to our *future* as they have been to our *past*. As such, along with the *Declaration of Independence*, they provide the philosophical basis upon which the *National Platform of Common Sense* is drafted.

WORLD WITHOUT END

The *Constitution* and its Amendments were drafted to establish *individual* rights and to *limit* the rights of government so as to prevent its otherwise inevitable transformation into a Monarchy or other form of blatant or veiled Dictatorship. The Framers' wanted to preclude a small group of individuals from establishing an elite status for themselves and their ascension to positions of power that would became more a right of ordainment than the result of an electoral process. The first three words were chosen with extreme care: *"We the People ..."* rather than *"We the Government."* It's not a question of *"which came first, the chicken or the egg"* or, in this case, *"which came first, the government or the people." "We the People"* came first! Perhaps the Framers knew something that many of us seemed to have forgotten: that it is *the People* who make the *government* ... not the *government* that makes *the People*.

Article I established the Legislative Branch (House of Representatives and the Senate). I do not think its placement was a matter of happenstance. I believe the Framers consider the Legislative Branch to be the cornerstone of the government in that its bicameral chambers (the House of Representatives and Senate) were, by nature, the elements of the Federal government most closely connected with *the People*. You may be surprised to learn that our Senators were originally selected by State legislatures (Article I, Section 3) rather than by general election until the 17th Amendment was passed in 1913. Few who walk among us were alive during those times. Remember that year, because it also marks the authorization of the Federal Income Tax (as per the 16th Amendment) … or to apply a President Franklin D. Roosevelt's famous quote to this different, but equally devastating scenario, *"… a date which will live in infamy."*

Article II established the Executive Branch and, with it, the positions of Presidency and Vice President. Article II, Section 1 originally provided for the Vice President to be whichever candidate received the second greatest number of votes in the Presidential election. In 1796, this resulted in John Adams winning the Presidency as a Federalist, but Thomas Jefferson winning the Vice Presidency as the Democratic-Republican Party's candidate (yes, it was the Democratic-Republican Party back then). It wasn't until the 12th Amendment was passed in 1804 that the Parties offered a *"ticket"* in which the Presidential and Vice Presidential candidates ran as an *"entry"* (to use a horse racing analogy). There's a part of me that wishes things wouldn't have changed. I can see it now: *"Ladies and Gentleman, now entering the Ballroom: President George W. Bush and perennial Vice President Al Gore."* Now, *that* would have been fun! Instead, the Vice Presidency has eroded into something more akin to the runner-up in the Miss America Pageant (*i.e.,* "a most important position …" of almost *meaningless* proportions unless something cataclysmic happens to the President).

Article III established the Judicial Branch of our government. Members of the Judicial Branch are positioned to be the *independent* guardians of the Republic. It is *their* responsibility, *without personal bias,* to determine whether the limitations of Federal power have been honored, whether the States *"play well in the sandbox"* together, and whether the rights of *the People* have been protected and preserved. In order to secure this *independence* from political or other influence, Federal judges basically get to serve in their positions for life or until they retire. That's why their appointments and confirmations are so *non-political* in nature and why their *personal* experiences (*i.e.,* biases) are never expected to enter into their decisions. The President in office just appoints the *best* and *most experienced* jurist available when an opening in a Federal court system arises. It's good to know that race, religion, gender, sexual-orientation, and political persuasion *never* enter into the selection process because, after all, *"Justice is blind."* Just as an aside: wouldn't it be nice to actually *get back* to this concept?

To digress for a moment: the Framers never meant for legislative appointments to be held for life. People took voting seriously in those days because, before elections, they didn't have a *voice* in how they were governed. As a result, their appreciation of *freedom* was significantly more intense than what may be common today. It would be beyond the Framer's comprehension to believe that someone would be *repeatedly elected* to a Federal position and potentially *serve until they die*. It would be equally beyond their comprehension to believe that someone could be elected solely because of *name-recognition* and *lineage* ... as if to *inherit* their office; that a candidate's *characteristics* might trump his or her *character*; that *expectations* might trump *experience*; and that *funding* might have more to do with which candidate was elected than the *foundational ideals* for which they stood. My, how times have changed!

Correspondingly, the Framers *limited* lifetime appointments to the Federal Judiciary. As has been discussed, this was meant to ensure impartiality and to establish a barrier to the inherent interference of special interests that might otherwise influence decisions. To wit:

"Our government's system of checks and balances gives the U.S. Senate a crucially important role to play in the judicial appointments process. The Constitution gives the president the power to nominate judges, but judges only get confirmed if the Senate decides they are suitable for a lifetime appointment and votes to approve them.

"The Senate is not a rubber stamp for the president's nominees-senators have a right and a duty to make an independent decision about whether a nominee deserves a lifetime appointment to the federal courts."

"Your senators need to hear from you—and they need to hear from you now. Write and call your senators and urge them to reject the (deleted word) *administration's court-packing plan. Tell them we need and deserve balance on the federal courts, not courts packed with* (deleted word) *appointees who do not reflect mainstream America."*

I share this quote with you because it is *directly* on point ... and also because it comes from the AFL-CIO's website at www.aflcio.org/issues/civilrights/judicialappointments.cfm (until it is taken down). The deleted words were *"Bush"* and *"ultraconservative"* but I'm sure they will update it to *"Obama"* and *"ultraliberal"* as soon as they get the chance.

Moving on: the Framers established the relationship between the Federal government and the States in Article IV; the *Constitution* as the supreme law of the land in Article VI; and the requirements for ratification of the *Constitution* in Article VII. Those are all well and good, but the one I skipped

... Article V ... is perhaps the most important; because it established how to *amend* the *Constitution*.

As you've undoubtedly noticed, I have great admiration for the Framers of the *Constitution* mostly because, unlike today's politicians, they didn't pretend to *know* everything. Their *acknowledgment* of their own fallibility was perhaps their *greatest* asset. Think about it: they could have made themselves Kings. Yet, they didn't. They also recognized the *Constitution* needed to be a *fluid* document that could be refined through *Amendment*. In my opinion, the *perfection* represented by the *Constitution* is best evidenced by its admitted *imperfection* and the process it defined to permit and even *encourage* any *necessary* Amendments.

The Framers' belief that any such Amendment should be *significant* and *well-reasoned* goes without saying. They rested the power with the representatives of *the People;* not with the retired generals, peanut farmers, former actors, baseball franchise owners, or community organizers who might someday be elected President, but with the Congressmen and Senators who are charged with the responsibility of representing *the People intelligently* and *without bias*. They also established high hurdles for passage: requiring either two-thirds of both the House and the Senate or two-thirds of the States to call for a Convention, plus three-fourths of both the House and the Senate or three-fourths of the States for final ratification.

The Framers also thought that the *Constitution* clearly established the parameters within which such Amendments needed to be fashioned to retain the Republic. They did not anticipate that Federal Courts would use their position as a discretionary platform to *make* law. Quite the contrary; they limited the Judicial Branch to *interpreting* the law. And to that point: those who are graced with an appointment to serve in the Judicial Branch of our government need to do just that ... limit themselves to *interpreting existing laws* rather than *making new laws*. If *new* laws are required, it remains the responsibility of the Legislative Branch to draft and pass them for review and approval by the President. Subsequently, if an issue arises associated with an *interpretation* of the *new* law, that facet shall remain the *exclusive* jurisdiction of the Judicial Branch. While this should not even have to be mentioned, recent events force me to painfully acknowledge the problem.

And as a reminder, the President is not a King, a Messiah, or even anything *more* than a citizen performing a role on behalf of the rest of us. He or she is a *civil servant* with a defined level of authority and a specific set of responsibilities. The President does not preside *over the People*, but rather he or she reports *to* them. The President is *not* vested with the power to decide which rights and privileges the government may wrest from its citizens; nor may he or she unilaterally determine what kind of social reform is required. The *Constitution* is eminently clear on these issues. *The People speak* through their representatives in both the House and the Senate, and it is the *President* who needs to *listen*.

As we attract candidates in each of the three Branches with an increasingly higher level of competence and a sincere desire to *serve* our country, many of our current issues will begin to disappear. In the interim, remember: *"Patience is a virtue."* So, may God grant each of us patience ... and do it *now!*

AMEN ... AMEN

I have a feeling that our Founding Fathers would have had a special appreciation for how Dr. Martin Luther King, Jr. concluded his famous *I Have a Dream* speech: *"Free at last! Free at last! Thank God Almighty, we are free at last!"*

It is within this spirit that I begin to offer the actual *National Platform of Common Sense*. So, let me set some ground rules:

There have been a lot of *"tags"* used to dismiss differing points of view. In the name of *"political correctness,"* our political Parties have effectively learned how to *shut down* legitimate debate by cavalierly accusing dissenting individuals of being members of ... or people who live in fear of ... a particular race, religion, gender, sexual-orientation, socio-economic status, etc. This flies in the face of social discourse, establishes emotional scaring, taints reputations, and creates a huge socio-political chasm in our country. And quite frankly, I'm fed up with it. So, I shall address it as a premise to all else which is discussed within the context of the *National Platform of Common Sense*.

CSC's Platform Position: This Platform *eliminates* the practice of *"political correctness"* and its use as a weapon for suppression. You see, *"political correctness"* damages relationships and ideologies over time. It identifies you with a group and then stereotypes *your* characteristics within the context of that group as it is popularly defined. Ultimately, this isolates members of the group as if to define them as a separate, and somehow less valuable, part of our culture. As a result, *prejudice* and *bigotry*

are *reinforced* ... *effective* communication is *shattered* ... and *NOTHING* ever changes.

If you need help understanding this proclamation, let's *"play the race card."* You can identify yourself as being a member of a particular race, but you'll inherently be saddled with whatever misperceptions society holds for your race until such time that society *changes*. With any luck, it will only be a couple of generations before that metamorphosis takes place. Unfortunately, you'll be long gone.

So, here's a news flash: the *only* race that should matter is that you're a member of the *human* race. If you conduct yourself accordingly, you'll go far. It isn't even hard. Just try following the *Golden Rule: "Do unto others as you would have them do unto you."* Don't want to be hated? Don't hate! Don't want to be cheated? Don't cheat! Don't want to be lied to? Don't lie! See how easy it is. If we were *all* too busy setting a *good* example, we *all* would be enjoying life *far* too much to be bitter and disappointed; and it's amazing how many opportunities suddenly arise when you follow this simple practice. Just apply this principle to the *"politically incorrect"* category of your choice.

For example: when it comes to religion, just *pick* one ... or *none*. The only restriction is that you can't try to impose *your* choice on others or use it as a justification to harass or harm others. Remember: *"Do unto others ..."*

As for sex: again, *pick* one! For that matter, try *both* if you're not afraid of surgery. If a scalpel makes you take pause, perhaps you should merely try a different wardrobe. No one but *you* should really care ... unless there are pre-existing relationships and children involved; in which case, if you were following the *Golden Rule*, you wouldn't have *created* the situation in the first place.

And when it comes to sexual-orientation: again, who cares? As long as you don't try to *impose* your choice on those who do not share your views on physical attraction, it's really no one else's business. I personally chose to *"come out of the bedroom"* a long time ago. I admit it ... I'm a raving *heterosexual*. Yet, my wife has gotten me hooked on HGTV to supplement my diet of boxing, football and MMA. *Now*, do you see why stereotypes can be so deceiving? Besides, if a same-sex couple wants to get married, more power to them. Let *them* participate in the financial and emotional mayhem associated with a legal divorce should they ever choose to separate. Why should *anyone* be exempt from intrusive, ill-conceived laws that ignore the reality that two adults have simply chosen to live their lives apart ... just as they previously chose to live their lives together?

Even socio-economic strata are not immune from the power of this proclamation. If you concentrated your time on living the *Golden Rule*, it is *extremely* likely that the world would come to know the *very best YOU!* You might even become rich (if you aren't already). As a matter of fact, I can almost assure you that you *would* be rich, regardless of your economic circumstances, because your *life* would be enriched ... as would the *lives* of those around you. And if you should suffer the good fortune of ... well ... establishing *"a good fortune,"* then you would have the opportunity to apply the *Golden Rule* once again to share your abundance with those who are *less* fortunate ... and to do so in a way that is *meaningful* to *you*; whether it be by gifting to your church, your school, a family in need, or a charity of your choosing. There wouldn't be a need for the government to decide *for* you; to redistribute your wealth ... as if *it* had the right or had earned the money in the first place. And *you* wouldn't need a tax deduction to encourage you to *"do the right thing."*

Perhaps, if this were how we lived our lives, we would be inclined to cry out: *"Free at last. Free at Last. Thank God Almighty, we are free at last!"*

ELECTION REFORM

ONLY QUALIFIED CANDIDATES NEED APPLY!

As the Common Sense Czar, I've elected (no pun intended) to start my formal Platform with *Election Reform*. If you've already read the two companion books that reflect upon the Democratic and Republican Platforms, respectively, you may have noticed that both go to *great lengths* to discuss how they'll *change* things. Now, if you think the system is as broken as I do, you probably searched feverishly for both Parties' concepts with respect to *Election Reform*. If you think you missed it in the Parties' respective Platforms, don't waste any time re-reading them. Both Platforms were essentially devoid of any meaningful reference to Election Reform. *"Why?"* ... you may ask. Well, it's because *both* Platforms were drafted by people who already *benefit* from the system as it presently exists.

As an analogy, it's like two people who only play *checkers*. It's a simple game with limited moves. Sometimes Red wins. Sometimes Black wins. Unless one player is *much* better than the other, the wins and losses balance out over time. It's like the Democrats are the majority, and then, the Republicans are the majority; the Democrats win the Presidency, and then, the Republicans win the Presidency. And when your Party is lucky enough to win the House, the Senate, and the Presidency all at the same time ... well, it's like having a bunch of *kings* when your opponent hasn't been able to say, *"King me"* ... even once (no pun intended).

Life is good, and you're comfortable with the game. Then, someone comes along and suggests that you use the same game board to play a *new* game named called *chess*. This makes you a bit nervous because there are all *sorts* of different moves for the different pieces ... and you have to really *think!* And, God forbid, they suggest a game of three-dimensional chess. You just don't have enough brain cells left from your college years to cope with *that* type of confusion. You feel threatened, so you refuse to play.

That's essentially why you don't see either Party really taking on Election Reform. Any meaningful change in the rules would force them to *think*. And we *can't* have that! But I'm the Common Sense Czar, and I can decree *anything* I *want* … and I *want* Election Reform. Why? Let's see. How about because the current system is insane!

<u>Natural Born Citizen: directed by Olive R. Rock</u>

Let's just focus on the Presidency because that will make our job a little easier and the rules are fairly clear. Article II, Section 1 of the United States Constitution defines the qualifications associated with the Presidency. It states:

> *"No person except a natural born citizen, or a citizen of the United States, at the time of the adoption of this Constitution, shall be eligible to the office of President; neither shall any person be eligible to that office who shall not have attained to the age of thirty-five years, and been fourteen years a resident within the United States."*

During the most recent Presidential election, both major Parties' candidates passed the age requirement. Senator McCain … well, I'm not sure *how* old he was because official records don't go back that far and the cave drawings have faded over time. But, suffice it to say that he was a busboy at *The Last Supper*, so he must have been over 35. A photocopy of President Obama's birth certificate (apparently obtained from some undocumented workers who normally just print driver's licenses) recorded his age as 47 old when he was elected.

As for the 14 year rule, Senator McCain was elected to the House of Representatives in 1982 and has served as a United States Senator continuously since 1986. President Obama worked as a civil rights attorney and taught constitutional law (believe it or not) at the University of Chicago Law School from 1992 – 2004. Also during part of that time, he was able to hold a second job; voting *"Present"* in the Illinois State Legislature from 1997 – 2004 while losing a bid for the United States House of Representatives in 2000. Until his election as President, he was able to log 143 days as a United States Senator after winning election to that chamber in 2004 following a stirring interaction with a Teleprompter at the 2004 Democratic National Convention.

The final hurdle was a bit more challenging for the men in question. You see, you have to be a *"natural born citizen"* to run for President. Just to be clear, *"natural born"* doesn't mean that you are precluded from running for President if you were born by Cesarean Section. What it does mean is a bit more complex. You have to look to the 14th Amendment in combination with Article 1, Section 8, Clause 4, which authorizes what has become Section 1401 of Title 8 of the United States Code. Confused yet? That's why attorneys get paid the big bucks ... and even *they* generally don't know what the law *really* says. In this case, it can be summarized as follows:

   a. Anyone born inside the United States and subject to its jurisdiction;
   b. Any Indian, Eskimo, Aleutian, or member of any other aboriginal tribe born in the United States, provided being a citizen of the U.S. doesn't impair or otherwise affect the person's rights to tribal or other property;
   c. Any one born outside the United States and its outlying possessions, both of whose parents are citizens of the U.S., as long as one parent has lived in the U.S. or one of its outlying possessions;
   d. Any one born outside the United States and its outlying possessions, if one parent is a citizen and lived in the U.S. or one of its outlying possessions for at least one year and the other parent is a U.S. national;
   e. Any one born in a U.S. possession, if one parent is a citizen and lived in the U.S. or one of its outlying possessions for at least one year
   f. Any one found in the U.S. under the age of five, whose parentage cannot be determined, as long as proof of non-citizenship is not provided by age 21;
   g. Any one born outside the United States and its outlying possessions, if one parent is an alien and as long as the other parent is a citizen of the U.S. who lived in the U.S. or one of its outlying possessions for at least five years (with military and diplomatic service included in this time);
   h. Any person born before noon on May 24, 1934 of an alien father and a U.S. citizen mother who has lived in the U.S. or one of its outlying possessions *(seriously, you can't make this type of stuff up).*

With additional provisions being applicable for individuals within territories acquired by United States over time, such as Puerto Rico (8 USC 1402), Alaska (8 USC 1404), Hawaii (8 USC 1405), the U.S. Virgin Islands (8 USC 1406), and Guam (8 USC 1407).

While Senator John McCain was born in the Canal Zone, he ostensibly qualified as a *"natural born citizen"* under 8 USC 1401(c): *"a person born outside of the United States and its outlying possessions of parents both of whom are* citizens of the United States and one of whom has had a residence in the United States or one of its outlying possessions, prior to the birth of such person." There is still some debate as to whether he actually *did* qualify under this exemption ... but he *lost*, so who cares?

Similarly, President Obama's citizenship remains a bit of an enigma. Some members of his political opposition have attempted to *"smear"* him just because the *"the Father of Transparency"* has never released his college transcripts, much less his original birth certificate. Why is either in question? Because there is some lingering doubt as to whether we was born in the United States (and more specifically, Hawaii). If he wasn't, he would need to qualify under one of the other criteria. At the time, his mother was a U.S. citizen but his father was a Kenyan. So, that pretty much rules out the more exceptional circumstances for qualification. Add to that the fact that Hawaii Revised Statute 338-178 allows parents to register a birth in Hawaii for a child that was born *outside* of Hawaii, as long as the parents, who for a year preceding the child's birth *claimed* Hawaii as their place of residence. Confused? Join the crowd! There's a concern that he may have been born in Kenya (or elsewhere) and that his parents then *registered* his birth as being in Hawaii, which would preclude him from being qualified to run for President. There are also a few other allegations involving name changes, multiple-social security numbers, and college loan applications submitted as a foreign student, coupled with his having spent over $1 million in legal fees to preclude the release of his records.

Do I necessarily believe all the speculation? No! Do I think a lot of time and money could have been spared by simply *releasing* all of the requested documentation? Yes! I think our *"transparent"* President was needlessly *"opaque"* in this regard; but then again in our current political environment, the new theme seems to be: *"Transparency is the New Opaque"*.

CSC's Platform Position: This Platform demands that if you want to run for office ... *any* office ... you have to release your records and provide proof that you *at least* meet the *minimum* qualifications of running as a candidate. It's just *"common sense."*

Let's take candidate qualifications to a new level. What if you were to create a *position description* for the Presidency (or any other political office)? What would the mandatory qualifications be? How about:

- Must be tall to project an image of executive stature
- Must be youthful in appearance to project an image of strength and good health
    - Must be willing to restrict smoking, drinking, and drug usage to private quarters *sans* press
- Must be reasonably good looking, if male, to *"sell"* well through all media
- Must *not* be good looking if female
    - Otherwise, all media attention will shift toward wardrobe, and all photos will be *"babe"* shots rather than thoughtful and discerning poses
    - Attractive female candidate will also not be projected as being capable of *intelligent* thought
- Must be willing to speak colloquially and roll up sleeves to appear to be *"in touch"* with the *common* people
- Must be able to read words on a Teleprompter with some degree of fluency
    - Stammering is permitted even to the degree that it causes distraction
    - Just don't mispronounce a word, or the press will treat you like you're a good looking woman … or a Southerner
    - Must be able to cite *"personal"* stories of constituents whom you've never met … as if they're close friends
    - Must have a few well-practiced mannerisms to pull out if needed (like biting your lower lip to express your emotional connection with your audience; feigning intellectual disgust as if everyone in the room is intellectually beneath you; and the *always* important ability to emphasize a point with the non-threatening, modified thumbs-up gesture)
- Must be alive and have no felony convictions … unless running as a Democrat
- Must be able to smile, shake hands, and kiss babies *ad infinitum*
    - Must be able to pretend to *care* while doing these things
- Must project an leadership image even if completely devoid of experience on a given issue
    - Must be able to use the power of the Office to bully and/or fire those with *far* more experience and wisdom in their respective areas of expertise
- Must not get caught in a compromising circumstance

- i.e., Must not be caught with a *dead* member of the *opposite* sex ... or a *live* member of the *same* sex
* Must be able to maintain plausible deniability under *any* set of circumstances
* Must be able to blame *others* ... for interminable periods of time and in a variety of subtle ways
* Must be willing to deny relationships with and/or fire long-time friends and associates if approval ratings begin to slip (including mistresses, religious mentors, associates who have tried to overthrow the United States government, and the occasional *"rogue"* family member)
* Must be willing to staff positions with sycophants and suffer working with individuals to whom you or someone else owes *huge* political favors
* Must be able to identify a running mate who is electable but is so inept that he or she serves as an *"insurance policy"* so that *no one* would ever want to have you leave office before the natural expiration of your term ... absent impeachment ... and maybe not even then
  - Special bonus points are awarded if you are blessed with a Majority Leader who is feared to be even more incompetent as a *"next in line"* than the Vice President
* And *absolutely* must be willing to say one thing while intending to do another

The following qualifications are not required, but preferred:
* Have something that sets you apart from the crowd
  - Be a member of a politically-active family ... or at least have the *surname* of one
  - If you're of mixed-race, be willing to ignore *one* parent's genes in favor of the *other's* based upon political expediency (*i.e.,* the combination of direct minority identification and the *"guilt feelings"* harbored by some non-minority voters)
  - Be a Nobel Prize Laureate, an Oscar winner, or invent something special (like the Internet)
  - Play the saxophone on *The David Letterman Show* or a guitar on your own show on Fox
* Have a spouse that believes that, when times get tough, Tammy Wynette essentially had it right: *Stand by Your Spouse*
  - Preferably without a history of repeated rehab

- Have cute, younger, photogenic children (preferably without arrest records) who can be *sedated* if necessary
- Have a dog
  - If you cannot afford one, one will be appointed for you by a court of law
- Be a clinically-diagnosed Narcissist or be able to demonstrate the equivalent experience
- Have a controllable level of attention deficit disorder
- Have non-controversial religious beliefs or a willingness to fake more mainstream ones, and
- Possess a broken moral compass to guide you when you're lost

These are all good, but in a country of more than 300 million people, shouldn't we be entitled to more? What about *real* world experience; demonstrated *leadership* abilities in *complex* scenarios; and an understanding of *finance*, *technical issues*, and *human behavior*? What about being *so* conversant with a *wide* range of subjects that you can speak fluently in an extemporaneous setting … without notes scribbled on your hand or the assistance of a Teleprompter? What about *attracting* and *retaining* the *best* experts our Nation has to offer *regardless* of whether they share your political point of view. Isn't it really about doing what's *right* for *the People?* Shouldn't leadership go beyond the ability to campaign? I guess that's why I'm not in politics. I obviously just don't understand. Then again, as the *Common Sense Czar*, I don't have to!

 **CSC's Platform Position:** This Platform calls for attracting the very *best* candidates that America has to offer. Let's not run candidates whose resumes would not even qualify them for consideration for a mid-level management position in a Fortune 500 company much less than as *"Leader of the Free World."* The Presidency, in particular, ought to be, in essence, a position based upon *"lifetime achievement"* ... like qualifying for a Nobel Pease Prize. Okay, *bad* example!

It would also be nice if the *first* President Bush would be vindicated on his assertion that *character* should matter. Bad character can end up being more than just a stain on a blue dress. It can be a *stain* on the Presidency ... or on the House or Senate. Surely, we can find people who are willing to behave with *honor* ... even if only for *one* term.

Similarly, the Presidency and Congressional seats should *not* be awarded to individuals because of *lineage* or *surname confusion*. We shouldn't just blindly vote for candidates because there is a "D" or an "R" after their name. It's every bit as *"racist"* to vote *for* candidates simply because they are of a particular race as it is to vote *against* them because of their race. It's every bit as *"bigoted"* to vote for candidates simply because they are of a particular *religion, gender,* or *sexual-orientation* as it is to vote against them because of their *religion, gender,* or *sexual-orientation*. And unless you only expect a candidate to accomplish a *single* objective during his or her term, you shouldn't make your decision based upon a *single* issue.

If you haven't researched the candidates' positions, let's just agree that you *won't* vote for *anyone* with regard to that position. In a Republic, the representatives *you* elect are *your* voice with respect to the direction *your* country will be heading. Either take the time to make an informed decision (rather than an emotional one), or *don't* vote on that issue. Trust me: if everyone would follow this premise, there would be enough *informed* voters to assure the safe progress of our country for generations to come.

And on a related subject, the West Coast has been featuring some interesting candidates in recent elections. Outside of retired actors, whose first political office has often been Governor of the seventh or eighth largest economy in the world, California has been running some accomplished business people against long-term political personalities. One race has pitted the former CEO of a Fortune 10 company with no direct political experience against a long-time political figure. Another has an individual, who served as CEO of a start-up that she took to Fortune 500 status (while not even voting in an election), competing against another long-time politician whose career has yo-yoed between former Governor of California ... to failed Presidential candidate ... to Mayor of Oakland. With such a wide disparity of backgrounds and experience, it may be difficult for some people to decide how to make a choice. Here's a recommendation. Which seems more ludicrous: having a former, successful CEO attempt to provide political leadership ... or having a career politician attempt to run a Fortune 500 company? It will force you to consider the actual, demonstrated talents and experience of the candidates rather than the political hype around them. As a result, their relative strengths and weaknesses will become clear, and your choices will become much easier.

♫ **MONEY, MONEY, MONEY, MONEY!** ♫

Fiscal Responsibility

Think about it. In the last Presidential Election, the Republican candidate raised about $368 million and spent $333 million. Not to be outdone, the Democratic candidate raised about $745 million and spent $730 million. Now, I'm not picking on Senator McCain or President Obama. I'm just stating fact; and the fact is the job pays $400,000 a year. It also provides a $50,000 expense account, a $100,000 non-taxable travel account, and $19,000 for entertainment. Let's make *all* the perks tax-free just for convenience and gross up the amount. That means that the President makes about $682 thousand a year. Not bad! Plus, you get to live in a *really* nice house that comes with a chef and gardener, as well as a cool car, a helicopter, and huge private plane (actually, two of them). So, to make the math easy; let's round everything up and say the job is worth $1 million a year *after* taxes.

That means that the winner paid $730 million for a job that pays $1 million a year. He'll only have to serve 730 years to break even! Of course, that's assuming that he gets around the Twenty-Second Amendment and wins reelection 182 times without ever having to spend another dime on campaigning. Hmmm ... are you starting to think like the *Common Sense Czar* yet?

Again, I'm not picking on President Obama. God bless him! I'm happy for him. But is there any wonder why we're in a *fiscal death spiral* as a country? I mean, the man spent $730 million to get elected to a job only pays about $1 million a year. Heck, if the Presidency pays anything *less* than $182.5 million a *year*, he *can't* recover the cost even if he serves two terms. So, that leads us to the following Election Reform proposition.

 **CSC's Platform Position:** This Platform *precludes* candidates from spending *more* to get elected than the *total* compensation provided by the position over its entire term. This would not only apply to the Presidency, but to House and Senate seats as well. Effectively, you can at best work for *free* ... but you *can't* spend *other* people's money to *buy* the position.

<u>Must Be Able to Balance a Checkbook ...</u>

Now, I know what some people are thinking. It's *not* the *candidate's* money; the money comes from *campaign funds* that were *specifically* raised to help the candidate get elected to office. So, the argument that the *candidate* isn't being fiscally reasonable doesn't apply. Actually, that's e*xactly* why it applies. It *isn't* the candidate's *own* money. It's money that belongs to other people. I am reminded of the sign in the Clinton campaign headquarters when he ran against the first President Bush: *"It's the economy, stupid."* To paraphrase: *"It's our money, stupid!"*

Notice that both Presidential candidates spent the vast majority of the dollars at their disposal. Senator McCain spent an absurd $333 million of the $368 million that was available to him. Did President Obama stop there? Certainly not! Because he *had* $745 million available to him, he spent almost *twice* as much as Senator McCain.

Why is this important? Because it demonstrates *how* these candidates will *likely* spend money in the future ... when it's not *their* money. Are you getting the connection yet? Our current candidates have been conditioned to spend almost *every* dime they can get their hands on ... and they have the power to influence the amount of taxes *you* pay.

Have you ever wondered why our country (or your State) can raise taxes to reduce debt, and yet the debt somehow mysteriously grows? Well, let me take the mystery out of it for you. When our representatives get their hands on *"fresh"* money, they find some other program they've always wanted to put in place and pass legislation to enact the new program. Of course, every *new* program needs a few *new* agencies these days; witness the 159 new agencies created by the Health Care Reform Bill. Now, compare that with President Franklin D. Roosevelt's entire *New Deal;* a complete social platform of historic proportions that created a whole 40 or so new agencies. Are you beginning to see the light?

CSC's Platform Position: Is it asking too much to suggest that our representatives demonstrate some *fundamental* understanding of finance? Can we *at least* demand that they prove that they know how to balance a checkbook; that they have a general attitude that they *cannot* spend *more* than they have and that it is *not* their *right* to just pass more taxes or print more money to assuage their insatiable appetite for spending? Deficit spending should be a last resort when *all* other options have been exhausted.

So, if you want to run in the future, this Platform requires that you demonstrate that you have exercised *some* sort of fiscal *restraint* and *responsibility* during the course of your lifetime; a time when you commanded *other* peoples' money and had to manage it *thoughtfully*. If you *can't* demonstrate that, you *can't* run`.

There are about 225 million adults in the United States, and we only need *one* President, *one* Vice President, 100 Senators, and 435 Congressmen. That means that we only need about 0.00024 percent of our adult population to serve ... or about one in every 419,000 adult citizens. So, do you think if we interviewed nearly a half-million people, we could find *one* who was qualified and had demonstrated fiscal responsibility? I think the odds are in our favor!

THE TERM-INATOR

Now that we've decided that our political candidates should actually be qualified for the positions they seek and that they need to be fiscally prudent, let's consider how long they should serve. It's really a choice between wine and bread. Do you think that your public officials *age* well over time; becoming richer in specific experience and more soothing to your political palette? Or do you believe that, like bread, they become *stale* if left in office too long; attracting parasites that grow on them until they only please their constituents' political appetites when offered with *"pork."*

You may have noticed that our *Constitution* reserves *lifetime* appointments to members of the Federal Judiciary to preserve their independence. No such luxury is afforded to either the Executive Officer or those members of the Legislative Branch because they are *expected* to be biased. President Franklin D. Roosevelt was beginning to test the waters of an eternal Presidency when fate intervened. Subsequent to his passing, the Twenty-Second Amendment was ratified stating that,

> *"No person shall be elected to the office of the President more than twice, and no person who has held the office of President, or acted as President, for more than two years of a term to which some other person was elected President shall be elected to the office of the President more than once."*

No such limitation is in place on members who serve the Legislative Branch. As a result, we have Congressmen and Senators who have served for *decades*. They attain senior positions, chairing critical committees, and rule with the iron hand of an insider. In some cases, no one can remember *why* they were put in these positions of power so many years ago, but no one wants to be the *"bad guy"* in removing them from their positions. It is left to the electorate to do the dirty work, and unfortunately, the electorate is generally uninformed and prone to displaying a habitual nature. Thus, we leave it up to God to determine when a former Klansman will pass away (*"He was just tryin' to get elected"* we will be told) or when an American *"icon"* will give up *"his"* seat.

Does any of this make sense? I think not! Are we so devoid of talent, that once we find someone who is narcissistic enough to subject themselves and their families to the mud through which they will be dragged, we will hold on to them as if they are our last hope? Again, I think not!

**CSC's Platform Position:** This Platform asserts that if we really want *"Change We Can Believe In,"* then let's try to attract some *real* talent to the political gene pool that can bring experience, wisdom, and fresh ideas to our government; talent that does not yet owe *anyone* ... *anything;* talent that has not become comfortable in the trappings that go with the office and ultimately create a sense of entitlement and elitism among most of our representatives.

The President currently serves a four-year term. It seems to take about a year for a *new* President to hit full stride. Then, the President is *effective* for about *two years* before ego gets in the way and the last year is spent running for *reelection*. If the President is successful in being re-elected, his or her *only* hope is to have a majority in the House and Senate or a *truly* bipartisan Congress (and *good luck* with that one in today's world). Otherwise, as a *"lame duck"* President with a recalcitrant Congress, he or she will be relegated to the level of ineffectiveness experienced during "W's" second term ... although a President need not *abdicate* to the degree that President Bush did.

**CSC's Platform Position:** This Platform calls for an amendment of the Twenty-Second Amendment to limit the Presidency to *one* term of *six* years. That way, we'll get at least *five* years of *effective focus* out of our President instead of two. Oh, I know what some of you are thinking: *"Six years! ... We can't even stand it for four!"* But the trade-off would be well worth it ... and there's *always* impeachment!

Along the same line, let's bump the minimum age to 55. Back in the late 1700's, 35 was a ripe old age. You may not have had a lot of years left. Today, 55 is considered to be fairly young, and I think we'd all benefit from a leader with 20 more years of demonstrated accomplishment. As the world has become increasingly complex, does anyone *really* think that a 35 year old *truly* has the experience to serve as the *"Leader of the Free World?"* If we choose to *leave* the age at 35, can we *at least* agree to require that candidates *can't* still be living with their

parents and that they must be able to demonstrate that they've *supported* themselves for five or more years?

And while we're at it, let's declare that the President cannot waste time and money on campaign trips for his or her political cronies anymore! Let's *really* reduce the carbon footprint the President has been leaving. Let's make the other candidates stand on their *own* merit. Let's not give in to the temptation to vote for candidates because we're in awe of the fact that they *appear* to be friends with the President. The reality is that they probably barely *know* the President. This is all *wasted time* and *money* to *induce* you to vote for the Party's candidate rather than the *best* person running. Take the time to *research* the candidates and *understand* what they bring to the table. You don't *need* a Party ... *or* a President ... to tell you *how* to vote. If you *do*, please *don't* vote!

Members of the House of Representatives serve two-year terms while members of the Senate serve six-year terms. Unfortunately, many of them serve until they are either *exposed* (sometimes in a *literal* sense) or they've *flat-lined*. Very little good comes from this. This is how a Republic can begin to drift toward a *different* form of government; how an elite class with a strong sense of entitlement can creep into our form of government. Telltale signs would include: private jets; *really* expensive offices; *ridiculously* large staffs that are more of an entourage; vacations in exotic locations (where our tax dollars are spent *outside* of the U.S.); special perks (like subsidized dining, haircuts, salons, beautiful exercise facilities, etc.); and maybe even *unique* health care and retirement programs (*exempt* from those which they apply to *us*) ... *for life*. Raise your hand if you think this could *possibly* happen in the United States.

Personally, I like the Senate's rotation. Every two years, *one-third* of the Senate is up for reelection. With the House, *every* seat is in play every *even* year. That's suppose to ensure that the members of the House are *"in touch"* with their constituents ... that they are *the People's* representatives. Again, raise your hand if you think that's what's happening. The reality is that House members are *constantly* running for reelection ... rather than doing the job for which they are elected. As a result, the average Congressman is elected to 4.5 consecutive terms and serves a little more than 9.3 years ... which means we probably squeeze about a month or two of *actual* work out of them during the time they're in office. I think the Senate's approach gives us more stability.

**CSC's Platform Position:** This Platform says, let's make it easy and pass a Constitutional Amendment that aligns *all* Legislative terms with our new found path for the Presidency; six-year terms … *one and out*. One-third of the House and Senate will rotate out every other year to keep fresh ideas coming. Six years will afford sufficient time to get things done without allowing other entities (like PACS, etc.) to gain any substantive level of undue influence. While that appears to extend the term of members of the House, it actually reduces them relative to what they currently average … and again, they can *always* be recalled if things get out of hand.

Unlike with the Presidency, this Platform shall permit members of the House and Senator to run for *additional* terms … as long as the terms *aren't* consecutive. If you're willing to sit out six years and then get back into the fray, good for you! *"Playing politician"* shouldn't be your life's work. You need to have time to embrace the *real* world. Otherwise, your political sensibilities may become skewed, and your sense of entitlement might be so profound as to allow someone to *"own"* your vote in return for their support.

Oh, and by the way, you *can't* alternate terms between the House and the Senate just to stay in Washington, D.C. When you finish your term in either the House or the Senate, you *still* have to sit on the sidelines for six years.

<u>*Anything You Say … Can and Will be Used Against You …*</u>

Political campaigns have become train wrecks. Ethics have gone by the boards. Campaign ads *smear* opponents more than having a bad wiper blade on a rainy day. Candidates can be *"bought and sold"* to the degree that you'd think that Reverend Jesse Jackson would be complaining. We need reform … lots and lots of reform!

**CSC's Platform Position:** Under this Platform, PACs, unions, companies, special interest groups, Hungarian-American currency traders, and for-

eign governments will no longer be able to *buy* a politician on the open market. Bribery is *not* a form of *free speech*. Neither will political Parties be allowed to *trade favors* in the form of other political positions to *dissuade* someone from running.

Only individual citizens will be able to contribute to a general campaign fund that will be shared equally among all qualified candidates (kind of like *"redistributing the wealth"* rather than having one candidate in a position to *grossly* outspend another). Each individual citizen *must* be *registered* to vote or they *cannot* contribute. This will stimulate voter registration as well as give us another opportunity to determine whether the individual is actually *alive* and *eligible* to vote.

The maximum contribution will be ... pick a number. Let's say it's $1,000 for Presidential, Senatorial, and Congressional campaigns (each). If all 225,000 citizens over the age of 18 register and scrape up $1,000 for each campaign, that's $225 million to divide up among the candidates in each of type of campaign. Since we've already decided that they can't spend more than they'd earn during their term (now, a uniform six years), that should be more than enough. If something less than 100% of adults *actually* registers and contributes, then it's up to the candidates to present compelling reasons why *everyone* should register and contribute. Otherwise, the candidates will need to learn to *balance* their checkbooks ... which isn't a bad alternative either. If they go *over* budget, they're automatically *disqualified*. I'll bet *that* will get their attention!

Since the FCC controls the airwaves, we can *mandate* a defined period of time for each candidate to debate or independently present their platform. This is not a return to the Equal Time Doctrine to the degree that it would infringe upon free speech or act as a suppression of the press, but rather it would a guarantee that *each* candidate would *at least* have the opportunity to be heard. So, Irishmen on Fox can still lust over the Conservative candidates of their choice, and *"softballers"* on MSNBC can still express their *tingling feelings* for Liberal candidates that give rise to such occasions.

This Platform also decrees that there will be no more *"dirty tricks"* in campaigning. If one of your supporters throws a rock through *your* campaign headquarters to generate negative press against *your* opponent ... your *supporter* will go directly to jail. They *do not pass "Go;"* they *do not collect $100*; and there is no *"Get Out of Jail Free"* card. We're basically going to have a *monopoly* on *the truth*.

All campaign ads must be approved by the *candidate* ... in writing; certifying that the *candidate* has seen, heard, and read whatever is applicable and *"approves of this message."* While third-party ads may be run, they must include a clear disclosure that the candidate has *not* approved of the ad and that it is being run *independently* (*i.e.*, something akin to notice on cigarettes packs: WARNING: THE *COMMON SENSE CZAR* HAS DETERMINED THAT THIS AD MAY BE HARMFUL TO YOUR POLITICAL HEALTH). If the ad knowingly contains *any* falsehood, the people responsible for producing the ad shall go directly to jail ... do not pass Go ... well, you know the drill. This does not restrict freedom of speech in that defamation and falsehoods are *not* protected forms of speech. So, let's put the burden squarely upon the shoulders of the candidates and those others who choose to express their opinions ... and if they endorse a lie, they go directly to jail, etc.

Moving on: a public record will be created that lists *every* promise that the candidates make and a scorecard of their performance will be published. Perhaps that will finally bring an end to the false promises that are made by pontificating candidates that begin with the infamous phrase, *"When I am elected, I will ..."* as if any of them really *has* the ability to *guarantee* anything! Maybe they will tone down their rhetoric to reflect that they will *"try"* to accomplish something in particular ... and we, in turn, will learn to limit our expectations to their sincere efforts. Since they can't immediately run for reelection anyway or serve a life term (at least in the political sense), maybe they won't feel so compelled to embellish upon the truth.

Imagine that: a campaign in which only the truth can be spoken and in which every candidate has an equal chance. Now, that's *"Change We Can Believe In."*

LEADERSHIP AND PROCEDURAL REFORM

A STAR IS BORN

In keeping with the current direction of *our* country and out of respect for the amount of debt we owe to China, I thought I would quote Lao Tse (in *Tao Te Ching*):

> *"The superior leader gets things done with very little motion. He imparts instruction not through many words but through a few deeds. He keeps informed about everything but interferes hardly at all. He is a catalyst, and though things would not get done well if he weren't there, when they succeed he takes no credit. And because he takes no credit, credit never leaves him."*

All kidding aside, that's a pretty profound description of *leadership* and one from which the *"leaders"* in our Executive and Legislative Branches would greatly benefit if they took heed. Compare and contrast that to their more predominant tendencies toward chest-thumping, credit-stealing, blame-shirking, and behavior-shifting. Am I the only one who's troubled by the *"star"* status that appears to be so desperately sought by our *"leaders?"*

I'd be more comfortable calling most of the members of the Executive and Legislative Branches of our government *"celebrities"* rather than *"leaders."* I think that would help the general public see them more clearly. After all, while we may misguidedly idolize *"celebrities"* for the roles or games they might play, we intuitively recognize that their importance is somewhat inflated and that their contribution to the world is one of *entertainment*. Celebrities help us separate our fantasies from reality by constantly being arrested or going into rehab. We are reminded that they are *not* what they appear to be. For example: in the series of very successful *Lethal Weapon* movies, Mel Gibson plays a *violent*, *reckless*, *borderline insane* individual who *only* gets along with

Danny Glover, his Black partner on the police force. It's *just* a character he plays in the movie! In real life, we know that Mel Gibson probably wouldn't *really* get along with Danny Glover. In a similar way, I think we should think of our current Executive and Legislative *"leadership"* as being more of an aggregation of *"celebrities."* It would spare us a lot of disappointment.

 **CSC's Platform Position:** Beyond the requirements already established in this Platform that mandate at least *some* demonstrated level of qualifications and fiscal acumen, this Platform also calls for a *Civil Service Test*. It can even be the same one that's given for most other Civil Service positions because it's really just a reminder that individuals who choose to run for President or as a member of the House or Senate are just that: *civil servants*. Maybe the humbling experience of sitting in a room and taking a test with *other* Americans will *remind* them that they should *only* be running for public office if they intend to *serve the People* ... rather than running for office because they believe the office can serve *them*.

A simple test might help in other ways as well. Witness Georgia's Fourth District Congressman who, during a committee hearing, admonished Admiral Robert Ward to consider whether *"the whole island* (Guam) *might become so populated* (if a Naval base were to be established there) *that it would tip over and capsize."* A Civil Service Test may have identified some other capacity the good Congressman could have pursued to serve his country other than serving as a member of the House. Then again, the Senate has a comic on board, so why shouldn't the House have someone who can make them laugh?

Just as an aside: Admiral Ward showed *true* leadership during the above mentioned incident. He maintained proper decorum and even managed to address the Congressman's concern with respect. Believe me, he deserves a medal. I know of few individuals who could have maintained their composure under fire as Admiral Ward did.

PROMISE THEM ANYTHING, BUT GIVE THEM OUR PAGE

I bring up Congressional Pages for two reasons. First, it helped me do a play-on-words with the old a slogan, *"Promise her anything, but give her Arpege."* Secondly, Pages answer the bulk of phone calls and mail received by Congressional offices. You'll almost never get through to your Congressman ... because they're *"stars"* ... but you *will* have the opportunity to speak with or receive a written response from a Page, who is a high school junior with a 3.0 or better grade point average (just our luck: Child Labor Laws preclude Congressional representatives from hiring 5th Graders). Now, why would you be contacting your Congressman, Senator, or even the President, anyway? Usually, it's because you're fed up with something. And that's where the *"Promise Them Anything"* paradigm arises.

You see, during campaigns, politicians will promise you just about *anything* to get your vote. Democratic candidates will make you feel bad about yourself so that you'll identify yourself with an *"oppressed minority"* for which they can create a stereotype. Then, they'll promise you *all sorts* of free programs (funded by taxes that will only impact the rich –which *you* can't be because you're *"oppressed"* ... and whom they'll condition you to align with Republicans). Conversely, Republicans will try to strike *fear* in your hearts that some people, country, or thing is *threatening* you in some meaningful way. Then, as the purveyors of *"truth, justice and the American way,"* they'll promise to *defend* you; all the while holding down costs and preserving your freedom. The reality is that both Parties *rarely* deliver on their promises. They're *only* made to secure your vote. For example:

In the most recent Presidential election campaign won by a Democrat (2008), the Democratic candidate promised (among other things):
- To close the detention center at Guantanamo in his first year
- To end the White House's hiring of former lobbyists into high-paying jobs
- To keep unemployment from rising above 8 percent
- To be completely transparent
- To disclose the names of all attendees at closed White House meetings
- To foster a new era of bipartisan cooperation
- To end all earmarks
- To broadcast the congressional health care negotiations live on C-SPAN

- To post all bills on the White House website for five days before signing them so the American public can see what it's getting
- To make peace with America's enemies abroad through direct, unconditional, diplomatic talks in his first year

In the most recent Presidential election campaign won by a Republican (2004), the Republican candidate promised (among other things):

- To capture or kill Osama bin Laden
- To restore honor and dignity to the White House
- To operate a fiscally conservative Administration
- To provide our troops with all the equipment and supplies they need to achieve victory
- To move Iraq toward self-government so we can withdraw our troops with honor
- To assure that every poor county in America has a community health center
- To offer a tax credit to small business and employees to establish health savings accounts and provide direct assistance to low-income citizens to help them participate
- To strengthen Social Security by allowing workers to save some of their taxes in personal accounts
- To protect small business from frivolous lawsuits
- To provide seven million more affordable homes so more Americans can enjoy home ownership

I rest my case.

 **CSC's Platform Position:** This Platform has already addressed this issue in part by calling for *"a public record (to) be made of every promise that candidates make and a scorecard of their performance (to) be published."* Its term limitation provisions will also help, since Presidential candidates won't get a second chance, and House and Senate candidates won't get an immediate one. They'll *all* have to build their legacies *during* the terms they serve.

But it goes beyond that. We need and *deserve* leadership. As the old saying goes, *"Say what you mean, and mean what you say."* That would be a great starting point. So, in the future, candidates will be *required* to speak more *specifically* about *what* they will do and *how* they will do it. Candidates will no longer be granted the literary license to speak in generalities. If you've got a plan, share it. If you don't, we're not interested in listening to you. The impact on the candidates and their Parties will be incredible.

Democrats will have to actually *explain* **how they're going to** *"save the world, eliminate hunger, cure cancer, and secure world peace"* **AND do the math as well to let us know how they're going to pay for it. Republicans will have to provide the** *details* **of** *why* **we'll all be** *"safer, happier and more enriched"* **by giving our votes to them and** *how* **they will accomplish their objectives. If this requirement was applied to the two Parties' last National Platforms, we would have saved a lot of trees, because there** *"wasn't a lot of meat on them bones."*

A POLITICAL *"END RUN"*

I encourage you to do a little research into what caused the collapse of Enron. A contributing factor to its demise was an accounting practice known as *"mark-to-market."* If you're not familiar with it, you'll get a real kick out of this one. In over-simplified terms: *"mark-to-market"* allows a company with outstanding energy-related or other derivative contracts on its balance sheet to book unrealized gains or losses to its income statement in order to adjust them to *"fair market value."* In the case of long-term commodities such as oil and gas, there may not be any *real* data upon which to base future valuations. So, you get to make up your *own* assumptions and models to *estimate* your earnings. The *really* cool thing is that you get to pretend that they're *real!* Essentially, Enron executives had the discretion to decide how much profit they were going to *theoretically* make several years down the road and *book* those projected earnings in the current period *as if they were a certainty.* Are you beginning to see where this FASB-approved practice might *"lead"* some individuals *"into temptation"* without *"delivering them from evil?"*

Okay, so we know what happened to Enron; fast forward to Washington, D.C., today. Our President and Vice President decide to try to make good on their campaign promises relative to improving the economy and reducing unemployment. Good for them! With the cooperation of the same brain-trust that brought us the Fannie Mae / Freddie Mac debacle that served as a catalyst to the recession in the first place, the American Recovery and Reinvestment Act of 2009 was born (a.k.a, *the Stimulus*). *Ta da!*

Pushed through as an *emergency* of *epic* proportions (of course, *all* due to George W. Bush's failed Administration), this nearly $800 billion program was directed at funding *"thousands of shovel ready jobs"* while reducing unemployment *below* 8 percent. It was positioned to *"create or save"* 3 to 4 million jobs. So, what does this have to do with *"mark-to-market?"*

Well, rule number one of *politics-as-usual* is: <u>Never</u> make promises that can be *tracked*. President Obama was new to his position, so he can be forgiven for *not* understanding the importance of this rule. Unemployment has risen *well above* 8 percent and the *"thousands of shovel ready jobs"* that were supposed to be around haven't exactly materialized. Apparently, only the rhetoric was *"shovel ready."* Luckily, the President still had a *"mark-to-market"* play: he said the Stimulus would *"create or <u>save</u>"* 3 to 4 million jobs. The *"creation"* part of the equation is a bit problematic. However, in true *"mark-to-market"* style, you can make up any number you *want* when it comes to *"saving"* jobs. It is in that light that the Administration has told us that 3-4 *million* additional jobs *would have been lost* had it not been for the Stimulus Bill. Basically, the President can throw out an estimate and say, *"Prove that I'm wrong!"* See how easy it is? Of course, it's more fun when you have someone like Vice President Biden deliver the news. Just sit him on your lap and have him tell the country how many jobs the Stimulus Bill has saved … just don't let anyone see your lips move.

"Mark-to-market" not only works with the Stimulus Bill, it works with *everything* having to do with Washington! Have you ever noticed how many programs either won't *begin* until the end of President Obama's first term or won't be able to be *measured* until *after* the end of his potential second term?

The $940 billion Health Care Reform Bill provides an overwhelming number of examples. While some of the costs and deliverables of the legislation commence this year, many of its *"improvements"* don't begin to go into effect until sometime in 2011 (the launch year for a Presidential re-election campaign) … or well beyond. Free annual wellness visits for Medicare beneficiaries and a new Medicaid program for poor go into effect between 2011 and 2014. These programs should be *implemented* (or at least *mentioned* during the campaign) … just in time to attract the votes of the effected *"oppressed minorities."* Enforcement penalties against individual families who choose *not* to be insured as well as companies with 50 or more employees …

which, when implemented, might *not* be so well received … go into effect *after* 2014 (*i.e.,* during what the President hopes will be his *second* term). The same is true for extending Medicaid coverage to low-income families, tax credits for low-income families, and the ability to buy insurance on state exchanges; all of which start sometime *after* 2014. If they don't happen, who cares? It's all about the President getting reelected.

And the projected savings that are expected to lower the cost of healthcare and reduce the deficit by $143 billion … well, that all occurs over a *ten* year period, by which time the President will be out of office and collecting huge fees for speaking engagements and his memoirs. If things *don't* pan out, it will *undoubtedly* be because his *successor* dropped the ball (just as it has been that every problem he has encountered to date has been the result of his *predecessor's* incompetence). Oh, and all those estimated savings … well, many of them are based upon actions being taken in the future that are *not* guaranteed to occur. They're based upon assumptions that had to be taken at face value by the Congressional Budget Office (CBO) when it projected the budgetary impact. Are you getting a better understanding of the practice of "*mark-to-market*" within the context of politics?

CSC's Platform Position: Again, while previous Platform positions will partially resolve this on-going problem (such as calling for *"a public record (to) be made of every promise that candidates make and a scorecard of their performance (to) be published"* and imposing term limitations), I want to be even more specific. In the future, this Platform will require elected officials, who propose legislation, to demonstrate fully-funded results within the context of their *terms;* and with respect to those officials who have the opportunity to run for a non-consecutive term, they will be banned from doing so if their sponsored legislation negatively misses its projection by more than 10 percent.

So, if you've only got a year left, work on legislation that can be implemented and justified within *that* year. If you have beneficial, longer-term ideas, share them with trusted colleagues who have sufficient time in office to implement them. It shouldn't be about getting *your* name on a piece of legislation … unless you think you're some kind of *celebrity*. It should be about doing *the work of the People* because you are, in fact, a *civil servant;* nothing *more* ... and nothing *less.*

YOU CAN'T HANDLE THE TRUTH!

Speaking of the Health Care Reform Bill, I would be remiss not to mention the need for *integrity* in leadership. There is a lecture I have given over the years that shares a philosophy in which I believe:

"There's no such thing as bad news in life. There's only reality. So, tell me the truth … and trust me to be professional enough not to shoot the messenger; intelligent enough to use our collective wisdom to reach a decision; and to believe in equity so that the decision balances the interests of all of parties involved."

Consider how it might have applied to the Health Care Reform Bill. We were told that the bill would cost about $940 billion and that it would reduce the deficit by $143 billion over a ten year period (and an additional $1 trillion between 2020 and 2030). Again, this projection is based upon the Congressional Budget Office's best estimate, which is again predicated upon the *assumption* that *everything* will occur *exactly as predicted* by the politicians. What could go possibly wrong with that idea? The magic number appeared to be $1 trillion. It seems that people still think $1 trillion is a lot of money … $940 billion is *much* more acceptable. So, the Obama Administration leaned on Congress to get the program under $1 trillion. At the eleventh hour, Congress was able to cut and paste a bill that got a $940 billion *"score"* from the CBO, and everyone rejoiced!

Now, we hear that the Health Care Reform Bill incorporated two new entitlement programs (insurance subsidies and long-term care insurance) whose cost assumptions weren't provided to the CBO. If that's true and the costs are as they are now projected, the $143 billion deficit *reduction* we were promised gets wiped out and replaced by a $544 billion *increase* in the deficit; not to mention that the $1 trillion *reduction* promised to occur during 2020-2030 becomes a $1.4 trillion *increase*).

While this is disturbing because the President promised that he would *not* approve the legislation if it would cost the American taxpayer even *"one thin dime,"* I don't know how he possibly could have known. The bill was over 2,700 pages and represented one of the most complex pieces of legislation ever drafted. It's not likely that he could have really *read* it much less *understood* it. He has a few other things on his plate. As I understand it, serving as the President might be even more challenging than serving as a community organizer. He probably had to take the word of his political cronies who were eager to *tell* him what they thought he *wanted* to hear.

 **CSC's Platform Position:** Again, you've probably noticed that previous Platform points are beginning to build a multi-tiered solution to many of the challenges our government presently faces. It's almost like the checks and balanced built into the creation of a Republic!

Attracting more qualified individuals to leadership positions and limiting their terms (to suppress temptation) are part of the answer, but this Platform wants to emphasize the importance of integrity. We don't need *sycophants* in office who only have the ability to tell us what we *want* to hear. We need *leaders* in office who have the integrity to tell us what we *need* to hear. Just *"tell us the truth and trust us to be professional enough not to shoot the messenger; intelligent enough to use our collective wisdom to reach a decision; and to believe in equity so that the decision balances the interests of all of parties involved."*

K.I.S.S.

You're probably familiar with the acronym K.I.S.S., which stands for *Keep It Simple Stupid*. Is it too much to ask to have the Legislative Branch embrace this concept? Since we've been taking about the Health Care Reform Bill, let's stick with that example; besides it contains just about every political sin one can imagine.

The Health Care Reform Bill is over 2,700 pages long. It was written by *one* Party, *behind closed doors*, with a number of critical votes secured by *pork*. So much for the President's campaign promises relating to bipartisanship, transparency, and open debate live on C-SPAN ... not to mention the elimination of earmarks. So, what can you pack in 2,700+ pages ... and what is the likelihood that a document that long and complex has *any* hope of being intelligently composed and tightly integrated?

Let's answer the last question first because it's so easy. There's virtually *no* chance that the Health Care Reform Bill is intelligently composed and tightly integrated. It's not like Congress took the time to put together an independent expert panel of physicians, nurses, hospital administrators, insurance providers, malpractice attorneys, and individuals with patient experience at a variety of levels who may have actually *had* the expertise necessary to identify and prioritize issues that could improve the efficiency and effectiveness of our health care system ... while reducing its cost. No, that would be *too* indicative of *true* leadership. Instead, we had Congressmen and Senators mulling over the issue ... when they weren't discussing whether Guam *"might tip over and capsize."* But don't worry, I have it on good authority that quite a few of them have stayed at a Holiday Inn Express ... at least before they became more elite members of our society as elected officials and began traveling on our tax dollars.

As far as what you can put in a 2,700 page bill ... well, one thing is for sure: *a lot* of pork! It would take about 1,000 pages to list the details for you, so suffice it to say that certain States such as Florida, Louisiana, Massachusetts, Montana, Nebraska, North Dakota, South Dakota, Utah, Vermont, and Wyoming did quite well for themselves and for certain constituents therein. Cosmetic surgeons also appear to have had a good lobbyist in their corner. Unions workers in given professions like longshoremen, electrical linemen, policemen, firefighters, EMT first responders, construction workers, miners, and people working in forestry, fishing and certain agriculture jobs *all* got *special exemptions*. A few community health centers and a small number of physician-owned hospitals gained special benefits if they were in a particular politician's jurisdiction, and it appears that AARP's lobby got what it wanted in return for its endorsement. Bottom line: we now live in *The Divided States of America*, where Federal laws apply in a disparate and disjointed manner and the cost is born by a select few.

CSC's Platform Position: **This Platform commands that, from this day forward, the Legislative Branch of our government must *"eat the elephant ... one bite at a time."* Complex issues must be broken down and presented for consideration in a cogent manner. Specifically, forget the Presidential *"line item veto"* concept that gets shot down every time it's raised. Besides, it could easily be abused by a political despot in that position, and it doesn't resolve the issue. Instead, if you want to draft legislation to address a particular issue within the context of health care (as an example), then that's the *single* issue upon which the legislation may focus. Related legislation can be presented separately and the interaction of the two bills can be explained, but they *must* stand *separately*. That way, when**

politicians who think that Guam might *"capsize"* have to vote on an issue, they *at least* will have *some* chance of *understanding* it? Over time, we'll attract more intellectually astute representation, but for the moment, we're stuck with the politicians that we unfathomably elected.

In addition, this Platform calls for each new piece of legislation to carry the name of the primary and secondary sponsors. Remember how the legislative implementation must be within the scope of the primary sponsor's tenure. Well, this also means that the responsibility falls squarely on that individual's shoulders along with those of any secondary sponsors. This takes us back to the *"scorecard"* I referred to with respect to campaign promises. A similar one will be kept with respect to sponsored legislation ... just in case sponsors want to *run* again after sitting out a term. Their records will be complete and on display for all to see. Only the *best* representatives of *the People* will be in a position to be honored with the opportunity to serve on multiple occasions.

As we move toward a greater depth of talent, our representatives will appreciate the restrictions I've placed on the legislative process. You may want to *"short"* political *"pork futures"* ... because they'll be no place to hide those types of programs. I think if we just *Keep It Simple*, it will help save all of our collective *"S's."*

FIX THE PROBLEM ... NOT THE BLAME!

"Fix the problem ... not the blame" was a phrase that I pick up from one of my most treasured mentors. I only heard him say it once, but it was so powerful that he never had to say it again. Wouldn't it be nice if our *"leaders"* accepted their roles as ... well ... *leaders!* In an effort to reinforce the previous section's K.I.S.S. concept, I'll get right to the point.

CSC's Platform Position: There's a phrase that's attributed to my favorite Greek philosopher, Anonymous: *"Yesterday is history, tomorrow is a mystery, and today is a gift; that's why they call it the present."*

Accordingly, this Platform calls for *all* political officials to live in the *present*. They should study the past so as not to repeat it (as per the advice of George Santayana), but they should remain firmly focused on the present ... to ensure us the best chance of *having* a future.

Because we have apparently evolved as a society, I can't call for cutting out the tongues of politicians who can only *"fix the blame."* Instead, this Platform hereby requires that those in office actually *do* their jobs. This is another reason the Platform limits the Presidency to one term, and the House and Senate seats to non-consecutive terms. Hereafter, political candidates will need to run *exclusively* on what *they* are going to *do* when *they* are in office ... and their promises will be tracked and recorded. As such, it will no longer be sufficient to run on the strategy that *"I am not my predecessor."* We already *know* that!

Also, once candidates get elected, they'll be *precluded* from explaining *their* failures on a basis of having *"inherited"* them. We all know someone who hasn't been blessed with particularly good *parents,* but it would be ridiculous for them to go around complaining about how their parents should *never* have been allowed to breed. The reality is ... they wouldn't *be* here but for that random act of passion. The same could be said for our political system: were there no predecessors, there would be no successors; and, as citizens, our circumstances are often the result of *"random acts"* of political *"passion"* without adequate *"protection,"* which make us feel as though we have been the object of some politician's unwanted advances.

So, from this day forward ... if you're going to run for public office, do so with the intention of *fixing* the *problems* rather than the *blame*; and while you're there, try to bring about *positive* improvements that reinforce *individual* rights within the context of our Republic. Now, that's *"Change We Can Believe In."*

IF WE PAY THEM, THEY WILL COME

I've talked a lot about improving the quality of our political leadership, but I haven't addressed the proverbial *"elephant in the room."* At the moment, we get what we pay for. So, we get a community organizer for President, a career politician as Vice President, and a frustrated cheerleader as Speaker of the House. This is our country's *Line of Succession* ... out of 225 million adults!

There isn't a company of substance in the world that would accept this scenario. Our President *might* qualify as an Associate Counsel given his legal background or as a low to middle-level manager based upon his potential. How quickly he would rise up the ranks is difficult to guess. Our Vice President might qualify as some sort of Public Relations associate. He has a nice smile and likes to talk. It's hard *not* to like him. Of course, he'd have to be trained not to get *too* excited about a *"big win"* for his company. In business, it's not considered professionally appropriate to refer to such accomplishments in public as *"a big f---ing deal."* And it's difficult to imagine our Speaker in a corporate setting. It would be easier to picture her well-practiced smile behind the reception desk of a cosmetic surgeon's Day Spa.

So, how do we overcome this? How about *paying* for the quality we need. I'm not talking about tens of millions of dollars like some CEOs command. For the most part, *they're* not worth that kind of money; they just have Boards and Shareholders that aren't paying close enough attention (but that's the subject of a whole other book). But I do think the *Leader of the Free World* is worth a few million dollars a year (maybe five). Senators are probably worth $1 million, and a really good Congressman might be worth around $500 thousand. Give them a tight expense budget, and if they go over it, the difference comes out of *their* pocket. That ought to bring an end to the worthless expenditures they've historically made because they didn't have to earn the money or account for it to the taxpayers.

I know what you're thinking. Won't this greatly *inflate* the cost of our Federal government? The answer is a resounding *"No!"* If you attract the right people who have *real world* experience, *know* how to lead, and have a *profound respect* for other people's money, the cost of government will go *down*. Serious times call for serious people; not individuals who are enamored with themselves and their own self-importance. Great people ... in positions of great importance ... recognize the value of surrounding themselves with other individuals who possess great talent. It's like comparing any of our incredibly skilled Special Forces units to a disorganized group of citizens in a combat environment; you don't need *nearly* as many of the highly-trained professionals as you need untrained *WANT-TO-BEs* ... to *"take the hill"* (no pun intended).

Picture our Federal government as the biggest, most important business in the world. Who would you want to lead it? Who would you want to work for? *That's* who we've got to begin to attract and get on board in Washington, D.C. And remember, it's not a long-term commitment. It's only for a *brief* (but *intense*) period of their lives. Then, they can go back to the private sector and pursue other innovative accomplishments that will improve the quality of our lives.

 **CSC's Platform Position: So, here it is ... a capitalistic approach to the Republic that should work in a free market environment. I think enough talented people will love this country as much as I do to give up six years of their life to serve the people. This Platform calls for the follow:**
- **The next President of the United States shall be paid $5 million a year and still get to use the great house, cars, helicopters, and planes ... *all* tax-free ... just *not* for campaigning or personal junkets. He or she will also be able to participate in the same pension and health care programs, etc. that are prescribed by Congressional legislation for citizens at large.**
- **The next Vice President of the United States, as President of the Senate, shall be paid as a Senator ($1 million a year) but get better perks (the use of the residence at One Observatory Circle as well as the use of the cars, helicopters and planes associated with the position, again, tax-free). He or she will also be able to participate in the same pension and health care programs, etc. that are prescribed by Congressional legislation for citizens at large.**
- **Commencing in six years, Senators shall be paid $1 million per year and will also be able to participate in the same pension and health care programs, etc. that are prescribed by Congressional legislation for citizens at large.**
- **Commencing in two years, the Speaker of the House shall be paid $500 thousand per year but, like the Vice President, enjoy a few nicer perks. He or she will also be**

able to participate in the same pension and health care programs, etc. that are prescribed by Congressional legislation for citizens at large.
- Commencing in two years, members of the House of Representatives shall be paid $500 thousand per year and will also be able to participate in the same pension and health care programs, etc. that are prescribed by Congressional legislation for citizens at large.
- Over the first six years of the transition, the President, Vice President, Senators and members of the House will be expected to identify at least a 5 percent reduction in expenses per year in their areas of control (30 percent over their term) ... just like business executives are challenged to do in the real world.
- Since, re-election is no longer an issue, all the time, money, and lost productivity heretofore wasted in re-election efforts shall be *immediately* discontinued. And the reduction in these individuals' carbon footprints' should noticeably lower global temperatures (for Al Gore and all you environmentalists out there).
- Similarly, office bearers will be banned from campaigning on behalf of *future* candidates while in office (what they do *afterwards*, on their *own* dime, is up to them). We're not paying them to be campaign managers or cheerleaders for some want-to-be dweebs. Either the new candidates demonstrate the capability to stand on their *own*, or they shouldn't be elected. Additionally, this will not only further lower their carbon footprints, but it will go a long way toward saving the chickens that tend to end up as the main course at most fund raising dinners (this is offered as a special *"shout out"* to all of my vegan friends and members of PETA).

And while it's a little off-subject, I'd like to address a related issue here rather than creating a separate Platform section for it. While our current politicians just *love* to fly around in their private or chartered jets or rack up frequent flyer miles while traveling on *our* dime (often inconveniencing other passengers or shutting down air traffic for hours as in the case of the Vice President's appearance on the Tonight Show in July of

2010) ... in the future, they can use some of the Internet technology that Al Gore undoubtedly invented to have *web-based* meetings. If you need to fire a General, either do it by phone, Skype, or by using a high-end system like one of HP's Halo™ rooms (if there's value to feeling like you're actually in the same room). Just don't feel the need to *fly* everywhere. It's terribly inefficient, it costs a lot of time and money, and it's apparently melting the polar ice caps. And maybe you can offer the *same* advice to the U.N. when it begins planning its next Climate Change Conference. I'm willing to bet that the American public would rather have you comfortably working from your *office* than flying around anyway ... since that's what they're *paying* you to *do!*

PROTECTING AND PRESERVING THE REPUBLIC

Now that we've cleaned up who's going to *serve the People* and the associated procedural issues, it's time to fix the mess that's been made of protecting and preserving the Republic. In fact, that's *all* I'm going to discuss going forward … because that's *all* that's really left. Everything else is a subset of that objective since the Republic, in turn, was designed to protect and preserve the rights of *the People*.

THE CONSTITUTION

The *Constitution* provides the framework for our Republic; a delineation of the specific powers and duties of the triumvirate of Branches that comprise our Federal government … and the reservation of all other *"unenumerated powers"* to the States and *the People*. As I mentioned before, I believe that Article I of the Constitution, which established the Legislative Branch, was constructed first for a reason: it contains the essence of the Republic. Sure Article II establishes the Executive Branch, including the offices of the President and Vice President, but while the President has the authority to veto Congressional legislation that is submitted for his or her approval, Congress can *still* override the President's veto with a two-thirds vote of members present. So, where's the *real* power? And while Article III established the Judicial Branch of our government, *that* Branch technically only has the authority to rule on whether legislation is constitutional and whether individual or State's rights have been violated. With respect to the law, *only* the Legislative Branch is vested with the authority to *make* it … or *remake* it if it is initially struck down by the Judicial

Branch. So, again, I'll emphasize that we must look to Article I for guidance when it comes to reclaiming our Republic.

Article I, Section 8, in particular defines the powers that the Framers gave to the legislative representatives of *the People* ... and the *limitations* they imposed upon those representatives. It defines in *specific* terms what the Federal government *must* do and, in *generic* terms, what the Federal government *may* do. As we will discuss, the driving force behind anything Congress might choose to pursue must be either for the *"common Defense"* or the *"general Welfare"* of the *entire* country. Correspondingly, it also effectively defines the role to be played by our State governments; limiting their scope of intervention to providing a more localized element of *"common Defense"* and the promulgation of services that impact the *"general Welfare"* of the citizens who reside within the State.

 **CSC's Platform Position:** Article VI of the *Constitution* provides:

"The Senators and Representatives before mentioned, and the Members of the several State Legislatures, and all executive and judicial Officers, both of the United States and of the several States, shall be bound by Oath or Affirmation, to support this Constitution; but no religious Test shall ever be required as a Qualification to any Office or public Trust under the United States."

Okay, if they are going to be *"bound by Oath or Affirmation, to support this Constitution"* they should *know* what they're swearing to uphold. As a result, this Platform calls upon individuals who aspire to run for a position within the Legislative Branch of our government to *read* the Constitution and pass a test that conclusively demonstrates that they actually *understand* it. Pursuant to Article VI, no *"religious"* questions will be asked (other than within the context of the *Constitution*) ... and if the test is administered on government property, we won't even allow the candidates to *pray* that they get the answers right.

Since this Platform has already prescribed steps for attracting a higher-level of candidate for every position, the testing requirement is not deemed to be unduly burdensome. And because it is limited to the *Constitution* and its

Amendments, it's automatically insulated from claims of racial, gender, and religious bias. Oh, and by the way, it will be administered in *English!*

And while we're on the subject, *all* candidates for the Presidency, Vice Presidency, the Federal bench, and any other position referenced in Article VI shall have to take and pass the *same* test. For those who are *already* in office: they must either *pass* the test ... or *step down!* That should help *"clean house"* (no pun intended).

Article II, Section 1 even spells out the President's *Oath of Office* (although certain Chief Justices are apparently unaware of this):

> *"I do solemnly swear (or affirm) that I will faithfully execute the Office of President of the United States, and will to the best of my Ability, preserve, protect and defend the Constitution of the United States."*

This seems eminently fair. After all, it has an exception for atheists who prefer to *"affirm"* rather than *"swear,"* and the attestation is only to act within the *"best of (your) Ability."* So, no matter *how* inept you might be, it's okay as long as you're using your best effort. The other important thing to note is that you are pledging to *"preserve, protect and defend the Constitution of the United States"* ... *not* to unilaterally *change* it. That protects us from narcissistic leaders who think that they might have to *mold* our country into something different than a Republic ... something other than the great Nation it has become.

TAXATION

As I mentioned, Article I, Section 8 prescribes how the Legislative Branch can fund its follies. So, in the spirit of *"Show Me the Money,"* lets start with the issue of taxes. Article I, Section 8 of the Constitution provides:

> "The Congress shall have Power To lay and collect Taxes, Duties, Imposts and Excises to pay the Debts and provide for the common Defence (sic) and general Welfare of the United States; but all Duties, Imposts and Excises shall be uniform throughout the United States ..."

It goes on to delineate other specific powers that are within the domain of Congress, but let's just focus on taxes at this point. It wasn't until the Sixteenth Amendment was ratified on February 3, 1913, that Congress secured:

"... the power to lay and collect taxes on <u>incomes</u>, from whatever source derived, without apportionment among the several States, and without regard to any census or enumeration."

Think about that for a minute. It took more than 125 *years* from the date the *Constitution* came into being before Congress deemed it to be *"necessary and proper"* to tax personal incomes. Yet today, it's as if it is *incumbent* upon Congress to find *new* ways to tax us ... and at increasingly *higher* levels. It begs the question, *"Why?"*

My belief is that taxes are one of the most effective ways to *control* the general population. It's not supposed to be that way in a Republic, but that certainly appears to be the case ever since the Sixteenth Amendment passed. Here's how it works:

- Voting requires behavior; you actually have to *physically* cast *your* vote (or, in *certain* quarters, someone *using* your identity votes *as if* they're you).
- To elicit the desired *behavior*, a *belief* must be in place (*i.e.,* you think Candidate A is a better choice for office than Candidate B).
- Generally speaking, your *belief* is based upon your *perception* that Candidate A possesses certain qualities, or represents certain interests, that you view as favorable to those possessed or represented by Candidate B.
- It's tough to articulate principles in a way that *everyone* understands them, so politicians tend to target smaller groups with a more common set of characteristics ... *"special interests"* if you will. Then, getting your vote is much easier because the politician has a defined set of characteristics upon which to focus that are likely to have an appeal to you.

As an example, a politician might identify a large group of people who rent apartments but would like to own a home. To target that base, the politician might begin talking about programs that promise to reduce the cost of loans and to lower the qualification criteria. Of course, this excites the members of that class that wish to own their first home, and they vote *disproportionately* for that candidate. Now, the candidate has to *deliver* on the promise, since under the current system, he or she probably wants to be a *career* politician. Of course, the people who *wanted* the program *can't* pay for it. If they could, they wouldn't need it in the first place. So, the politician places the burden on a *different* group of citizens. The default solution is to tax the *"rich"* (however *"rich"* may be defined). As long as the definition doesn't include *you*, why should you care?

Remember the discussion about *why* the Framers didn't create a Democracy? This is a classic example of *why*. But the candidate got elected, and after all, that's the real *"end game."*

So, in summary: the candidate appealed to a select group's special interests and was *perceived* to *care* about them; a belief was formed based upon the desired perception that the candidate created; the belief led to the desired behavior (a vote for the candidate); and in a perfect world, the candidate *actually* delivered on the promise ... and paid for it by taxing a smaller group of citizens with less voting power. *Everyone* wins ... except for the Republic and the people paying the tab ... and yet one *more* sense of *"entitlement"* is established.

The Framers suffered great hardships to come to the *New World* to carve out an existence. They rejected *"taxation without representation,"* and it is unlikely that they would support a *"redistribution of wealth"* if they were alive today. We're talking about people like Benjamin Franklin, who's famous for saying, "*A penny saved is a penny earned*" ... *"Time is money"* ... *"Rather go to bed without dinner than to rise in debt."* Do you *really* think that he or any of his peers were into *"redistributing wealth"* beyond the concept of charitable giving? And the reality is that income taxes have been misapplied since their inception to *"redistribute wealth."* It isn't a particularly new concept and it isn't tied to one Party. It's been around for years. It just happens that the phrase has become more popular and represents one of the few instances in which the current Administration has made good on its promise to be more *"transparent."*

 **CSC's Platform Position:** Once again, by attracting higher-quality, term-limited candidates, who can balance a checkbook, this Platform hopes to mitigate the candidates' tendency to *"game"* people for votes and to unjustly punish others (through the advent of taxes) for the transgressions of their campaign promises.

Destroying the Field of Dreams

"If we have it, we will spend it." That seems to be the mantra of our Legislative Branch of government. As a corollary, we can add the Democratic dogma: *"If we don't have it, we will spend it anyway."* In the past, the power to tax has been the *secret weapon* of *both* Parties. Democrats use it to get votes by promising to only tax the rich to fund programs for everyone else. Republicans use it to get votes by claiming that they will *protect* the public against pernicious taxation. Here's the reality:

Republican candidates routinely promise that they're not going to raise taxes … not on *you* as an individual or on *businesses* in general (one of their few reliable constituencies) … because taxes negatively impact the economy. *"Read my lips … no new taxes."* It's a *clear* and *intentional* misrepresentation. If cutting taxes stimulates the economy, why not eliminate *all* taxes? Oh, yeah … then we couldn't pay for government salaries, perks, offices, boondoggle trips, etc. Scratch that idea! I guess *some* taxes are okay. But the one thing about Republicans is that they can do the math. If they can't pay their debts, they'll *raise* your taxes *regardless* of what they've promised. They just do it under the guise of *necessity*.

The Democrats are far more forthright on this issue. They're going to raise your taxes under *any* circumstances because they're sure they can create *some* kind of social program to spend the money … no matter *how* much is available. Normally, this would turn off a lot of people, but the Democrats *always* promise to *only* tax the rich. Robin Hood would be so proud! You see, the *rich* are really just like the Sheriff of Nottingham who, as we all know, wrongfully took money from the poor by abusing his power … kind of like Congress does.

And when the Democrats promise to *only* tax the rich … well, that's *"Change We Can Believe In."* For example: when President Obama raised the cigarette tax 62 cents per pack just about a month after taking office, I was all for it. You see, I *don't* smoke … and even if I *did* … I'm *not* rich! I'm feeling totally Democratic about this one. Apparently, only the rich smoke. Either that … or the President was just *"blowing smoke"* when he promised not to raise taxes on anyone making less than $250 thousand a year. But who could accuse him of that when he sets an appropriate example for the rest of us by smoking *and* earning more than $250 thousand a year. That's stepping up to the plate!

Correspondingly, when President Obama was running against President Bush (let's face it, he might as well have been since that was the *entire* basis of his campaign), he excoriated the former President for presiding over a $2.5 trillion expansion of our national debt (which, by the way, President Obama *voted* for when he was in the Senate). Then, as soon as he took office, he essentially doubled that level of expansion. With this level of spending, President Obama will be hard pressed to keep his campaign promise to *only* increase taxes on the *richest* 5 percent of our population while *reducing* taxes for everyone else ... *unless* there is an expansion of the money supply. Our inability as voters to recognize the mathematical certainty of this demonstrates why so few contestants ever win on the game show *Are You Smarter than a Fifth Grader*? As a result, you can expect the government to increase the money supply to close the gap.

Now, since our currency isn't really *backed* by anything (we went off the gold standard back in 1975), expanding the cash supply really doesn't hurt us in any way ... *unless* you consider the impact of inflation. You see, if the government prints a lot of money to pay for all of the new social programs and agencies that it's putting in place, the law of supply and demand suggests that, as the monetary supply grows, the dollar will be devalued. So, something that costs a dollar today will cost *more* than a dollar tomorrow if everything adjusts to stay the same (*i.e.,* to maintain the dynamic equilibrium of the economy). Luckily, this will *only* impact the richest 5 percent of our population since President Obama *promised* that only *they* would suffer a tax increase.

Now, why do I say that? Well, taxes are just a method of paying for government programs. If the money supply has to be manipulated to pay for government programs, isn't the resultant inflation, in effect, a tax? I can't wait to see how President Obama makes sure that only the food, drink, housing, clothing, etc. of the *rich* gets adjusted for inflation. Otherwise, he will have broken his promise to 95 percent of Americans who *thought* they were getting the deal of the century! I can see it now: I'll be going through a checkout line, and the clerk will ask me to produce some sort of National Identification card that will let him or her know that I'm not one of the top 5 percent. Bingo! I'll either get a discount, or I'll get to avoid paying a premium since we've been promised that *all* these new programs will *only* impact the pocket books of the rich. Either way, it's good to know that most of us will be insulated against the effect of runaway inflation.

 **CSC's Platform Position: The best way to destroy the *"Field of Dreams"* mentality that is so prevalent in Washington, D.C. is to restrict *Congress'***

cash flow ... as was intended by the Framers when they spelled out the limitations relative to the Legislative Branch's *"Power To lay and collect Taxes, Duties, Imposts and Excises"* in Article I, Section 8. So, this Platform requires Congress to follow the Constitution as it was written.

Since this Platform has already called for a Constitutional Test to be administered to (and passed by) all candidates and existing Federal officials, there will be *no* excuse going forward that they *"just didn't know."* And by attracting higher-quality, term-limited candidates, who take responsibility for their decisions and respect the limitations within which they can *justify* a program and collect *taxes* to pay for it, this Platform hopes to *"Destroy the Field of Dreams"*

<u>Nothing is Certain but Death and Taxes</u>

What's all the debate over the Progressive Tax, Flat Tax, and Value-Added Tax concepts? Today, we have a Progressive Tax in place. The more you make, the more you pay. The *harder* you work, the *less* you get to keep. It's only fair!

Do you remember the fact that the Framers of the Constitution elected to create a *Republic* rather than a *Democracy*? Again, *this* is one of the reasons why. President Obama has done this country a great service by drawing a clear line in the sand to distinguish the *We's* from the *They's*. He's theoretically pitted 95 percent of the population against the other 5 percent. Guess who's going to win *that* vote in a Democracy? The Framers recognized this weakness and protected against it by forming, as Benjamin Franklin prophetically declared, *"A Republic, if you can keep it."*

It's the second part of Franklin's statement that can be difficult, and *this* is one of those times. Sure, 95 percent of the people may think that the current Administration's plan is just *fine* ... but is it *right?* Marxism, Communism, and Socialism all call for a *"redistribution of wealth"* and support the concept of a *single class* of citizens; but a Republic does *not*. To quote the Declaration of Independence:

"We hold these truths to be self-evident, that all men are created equal, that they are endowed by their Creator with certain unalienable Rights, that among these are Life, Liberty and the pursuit of Happiness."

While under the Republic we are all deemed to have been created *equal* and to have the right to live and be free, we also have the right to *pursue* happiness rather than to be given it. For that is part of our freedom: the right to explore and select from among *many* alternatives based upon our interest, our desires, and our willingness to invest and profit from our *own* efforts. There is *nothing* in our history to suggest that our Founders *ever* intended to create a society in which unequal efforts should generate equal rewards. The Progressive Tax is merely a manifestation of Franklin's fear that we may not be able to *"keep"* the Republic.

Remember that the top earning 5 percent of our citizens currently pay in excess of *60 percent* of the total taxes collected by the United States Government, while the bottom earning 50 percent of our citizens pay less than *3 percent* of the taxes that keep this country running (with about 40 percent of our citizens paying *no* taxes whatsoever). That's what a Progressive Tax does ... in the name of *fairness*.

Even a Flat Tax does *not* create complete equity. It does not create a *uniform* cost of citizenship (*i.e., "X"* dollars per person). Instead, a Flat Tax merely calls upon everybody to pay the *exact same percentage*. Let's use 25 percent as an example. If a rich person *earns* $250,000 and pays 25 percent, he or she pays $62,500 in taxes and takes home $187,500. If someone else earns $25,000 and pays 25 percent; he or she pays $6,250 in taxes and takes home $18,750. So, the person earning ten times more *pays* ten times more.

A Value-Added Tax (VAT) is somewhat of a blend. In theory, it would apply a uniform tax rate (in the form of a percentage) to the *"sale"* of both goods and services. Since rich people have more disposable income, they tend to buy more goods and services. As a result, they would pay a more progressive share for their citizenship than individuals with less income. The problem with a VAT is that governments in other countries tend to tack it on to already *existing* income tax structures, ostensibly to help make a *"correction"* in their economies. The reality is that these taxes are almost *never* discontinued when administered that way, and it is unlikely that it would be any different in our country. VATs simply become a perpetuated addition to the tax base, and politicians create entitlement programs based upon the continued availability of these funds. *"If we have it, we will spend it."*

CSC's Platform Position: Some of the issues that contribute to the national debt have already been addressed by previous Sections of this Platform. First, if we only let fiscally responsible candidates run for public office, much of the problem goes away. These

people will know how to function within a budget. Secondly, by imposing term limitations for the Presidency and a limitation on consecutive terms for members of the House and Senate, a lot of the motivation to create needless entitlement programs will go away. It's sort of like a self-cleaning oven. When you close the door on creating a career in politics, it turns up the heat to do the right thing when you're in office and bakes away the urge to promise whatever it takes to get re-elected ... since you can't.

This Platform also calls for the introduction of an indexed budget for Congress; whether it be indexed to the Gross Domestic Product (GDP), the number of citizens in the United States, or some other blended formula that relates to the size of our economy and our population base. As our country expands or contracts in both terms of its economy and population, so should the government's budget in proportion thereto. Other than in times of an unexpected national emergency (*e.g.,* a war, *legitimate* pandemic, terrorist attack, etc.), there would be no other way to infuse the government with money (other than by utilizing past budgetary surpluses); *no* additional taxation, *no* printing of money ... *nothing!* The country's over-draft protection could begin with a proportionate reduction in the wages of the Federal government. Since *they're* in control of their spending on *our* dime, *they* should feel the pinch first. Thus, marks the end of *La Dolce Vita.*

Beyond that, as much as I like the idea of a single, Value-Added Tax because it's tied *directly* to the economy and would obsolete the need for much of the Internal Revenue Service and completely eliminate the need for me to ever file another tax return, I don't see that happening. So, this I'm going to throw my hat into the ring for a Flat Tax that would make the Framers proud, and maybe we can achieve some of the other goals in a creative way. As a result, this Platform suggests the following:

- Let's determine what would be a reasonable indexed operating budget for the government and work backwards from there to calculate the correct percentage to apply to everyone ... *equally.* If you don't have any income of any

kind, you don't pay any taxes. Otherwise, we'll *all* have the same skin in the game.
- Let's simplify the process while we're at it. First, let's eliminate *all* of the deductions (both business and personal). That will streamline the calculation. And don't worry about what will happen when you lose the deductions that you've grown to view as an entitlement. In all actuality, they're merely tools by which politicians manipulate us. Remember: we're working backwards when we do the math, so the infusion of tax dollars from the elimination of deductions will help reach the budgetary objective *sooner* and, in turn, will reduce the overall percentage that you'll be charged.
- The elimination of deductions should help in a variety of ways. Individual and business decisions will become more legitimately based. Charity may even return to the heart rather than emanate from the tax return. Millions of trees will be saved. How, you ask? Well, if Congress doesn't spend a lot of time adding thousands of pages to each bill it drafts to account for the special interests it panders to through tax deductions and credits, millions of trees will be saved. This could be the environmental solution of our lifetime. Members of the Green Party ... *Unite!*
- Similarly, if Congress is limited to a single way of generating tax revenues, just think of how much *time* and *money* will be *saved* and how that *time* and *money* can be *redirected* to *important* issues ... rather than on the negotiation of backroom deals and the distribution of pork. IRS staffing can be reduced; the *"business of the People"* can be properly addressed; and even insane, scare-tactic ads for tax services might stop running on TV (*i.e.*, *"Are you being audited? Have you not filed tax returns for years? Is the IRS coming to your home or place of business? The IRS will relentlessly pursue you for unpaid taxes!"* – Gee, go figure!)
- Businesses will pay upon the *distribution* of both passive and active income. They will reserve the appropriate percentage on *any* distributed income and pay that sum to the government according to a uniform schedule. As a result,

individuals will *no longer* have to file any kind of income tax form. How terrific will that be? (Sorry, H&R Block!) And to mitigate the chance of misconduct, the penalties for improper reporting will be swift and significant (including fines and imprisonment).

• If we begin to elect the right people and they manage to operate the country under the indexed budget, at least some percentage of the surplus can either be *returned* to *you* as a taxpayer (since it's *really* your money) or the tax rate can be *adjusted downward* for *everyone* ... similar to the way an accrued mortgage payment may fluctuate as taxes or insurance premiums change over time.

Well, that's enough for starters. Besides, that's *a lot* more *detail* than you normally get in a political Platform. The beauty is that it's clean, simple to administer, and treats *everyone* fairly. Yes, there is a *"price of admission"* to be a citizen of the United States; *no one* gets a *"free ride."* As a collateral benefit, your vote can no longer be *bought* by political promises. Welcome back to the Republic!

THE LEGISLATIVE CHARTER

Now that we've addressed how money may be *raised*, I think it's appropriate to see upon what basis it can be *spent*. Let's return to Article I, Section 8:

"The Congress shall have Power To ... lay and collect Taxes, Duties, Imposts and Excises ... to pay the Debts ... and provide for the common Defence (sic) and general Welfare of the United States; but all Duties, Imposts and Excises shall be uniform throughout the United States; ..." (parsed to separate each relevant element).

 **CSC's Platform Position: For starters, this Platform proclaims that Congress can collect money to: (1) pay debts; and (2) provide for the *"common Defense"* and the *"general Welfare of the United States."* It can do this as long as it collects such money in a *"uniform"* manner. Notice that the word *"Welfare"* is preceded by the word *"general"* and is used in conjunction with *"common Defense."* Other than for the political expediency of**

radically broadening the interpretation of these specific words (of which Alexander Hamilton was a proponent until Aaron Burr put him out of his misery in a duel), the words themselves reflect a *limitation* on Congress' power to raise money; a limitation tied to *"common"* and *"general"* benefits associated with the *"Defense"* and *"Welfare"* of *"the United States"* (*i.e., all* of *the People* ... rather than some subset thereof).

I don't see anything about collecting money to *"redistribute the wealth"* or to fund special interest programs beyond the *"common"* and *"general"* interest of *the People* at large. Nor do I see anything in the language that would allow pork-barrel exemptions to it. Presidents James Madison and Thomas Jefferson, who had a bit to do with the conceptual underpinnings of our Nation, apparently concurred with my somewhat strict interpretation of the language.

And as we've already discussed, the Sixteenth Amendment gave Congress the additional power to tax income. However, it didn't expand the *purposes* for which the Federal government could incur *costs* or assume *debt*. It merely gave rise to a new source of funds with which it could *pay* such costs and retire such debts.

As a result, this Platform recommends refocusing on what the Constitution actually *says* rather than *embellishing* upon it for the sake of appeasing the insatiable appetite for power that has apparently infected *each* of the three Branches of our government over the years.

Now, let's continue with the specific responsibilities delegated to the Legislative Branch under Article I, Section 8, and I'll annotate each section as we go: *Congress shall have Power ...*

- *"To borrow money on the credit of the United States;"*

     **CSC's Editorial Comment:** We had no problem jumping on *this* bandwagon.

- *"To regulate Commerce with foreign Nations, and among the several States, and with the Indian Tribes;"*

 **CSC's Editorial Comment:** Again, we had no problem in this area either since money was involved.

- *"To establish an (sic) uniform Rule of Naturalization, and uniform Laws on the subject of Bankruptcies throughout the United States;"*

 **CSC's Editorial Comment:** We've *established* a *uniform* Rule of Naturalization. Our politicians just don't like to *enforce* it because it would jeopardize certain voting blocks they need to get elected. So instead, we *spend* taxpayer money to *sue* States that try to protect their citizens by *enforcing* the Federal law that's already in place.

Until recently, a *uniform* Bankruptcy Law had also been well established. However, once again, our politicians recognized an opportunity to nationalize a heavily unionized industry (the Automotive industry), ostensibly to *avoid* bankruptcy; only to have the related businesses file for bankruptcy *after* a significant share of *ownership* had been transferred to ... you guessed it ... the union. Hmmm? You don't suppose that politics had anything to do with this, do you? Other than with respect to *"special circumstances"* like this *(i.e.,* where *serious* political capital is in play), it appears that the law is still in tact with respect to the *rest* of us.

- *"To coin Money, regulate the Value thereof, and of foreign Coin, and fix the Standard of Weights and Measures;"*

 **CSC's Editorial Comment:** Our politicians are all over the coining of money and regulation of its value. Can you spell *"POWER?"* However, I suspect that they couldn't care less about the Standard of Weights and Measures ... because there's no real money in it.

- *"To provide for the Punishment of counterfeiting the Securities and current Coin of the United States;"*

 **CSC's Editorial Comment:** Again, if money is involved, you can rest assured that it's been a priority for our politicians.

- *"To establish Post Offices and Post Roads;"*

 **CSC's Editorial Comment:** Our politicians have repeatedly shown how a government-run business can compete successfully with the private sector. They've demonstrated an amazing ability to source Post Offices, Post Roads ... and *Post Turtles*. I can't wait until the government enters the health insurance business. If the United States Postal Service provides any insight, just imagine what direction the quality and cost of our health care will go.

- *"To promote the Progress of Science and useful Arts, by securing for limited Times to Authors and Inventors the exclusive Right to their respective Writings and Discoveries;"*

 **CSC's Editorial Comment:** The government can generate cash through patent and trademark applications, so you can mark this one *"under control."* The fact that it takes a ridiculously long time to *get* a patent (so much so that a *new* technology might emerge between applying for a patent and the actual issuance of one) is just one more tribute to the efficiency of government-run organizations.

- *'To constitute Tribunals inferior to the supreme (sic) Court;"*

 **CSC's Editorial Comment:** There are days when it seems difficult to comprehend creating Tribunals that are *"inferior"* to the Supreme Court, but I suspect that the Framers meant a system of lower

courts ... rather than using the word *"inferior"* for comparative purposes.

- *"To define and punish Piracies and Felonies committed on the high Seas, and Offenses against the Law of Nations;"*

 **CSC's Editorial Comment:** With piracy and terrorism at all-time highs, we do a good job of hunting down and capturing those who are suspected of such heinous crimes. However, with the intervention of *"political correctness,"* our view of acceptable punish is now restricted to providing such prisoners with only 3-star accommodations, basic cable, and cheap Chardonnay served at room temperature.

- *"To declare War, grant Letters of Marque and Reprisal, and make Rules concerning Captures on Land and Water;"*

 **CSC's Editorial Comment:** We can still wage War. However, our rules of engagement have once again been modified due to *"political correctness."* I could be wrong, but I believe the latest version is that you cannot *fire* at suspected enemy combatants until they have *killed* you.

- *"To raise and support Armies, but no Appropriation of Money to that Use shall be for a longer Term than two Years;"*

 **CSC's Editorial Comment:** I believe we actually adhere to this one.

- *"To provide and maintain a Navy;"*

 **CSC's Editorial Comment:** We're on a roll! We do this one too.

- *"To make Rules for the Government and Regulation of the land and naval Forces;"*

CSC's Editorial Comment: There's no stopping us. We do this one too! Of course, this is also where our *"kinder and gentler"* rules of engagement are empowered; but at least we won't have to apologize for our arrogant behavior as much in the future. I'm sure the extra coffins and flags will be a small price to pay for being viewed as *"politically correct"* by those whom we wish to impress abroad.

- *"To provide for calling forth the Militia to execute the Laws of the Union, suppress Insurrections and repel Invasions;"*

CSC's Editorial Comment: Again, no problem … although we prefer that they just *volunteer*. If only we can keep the economy in the tank, more people will *have* to volunteer to serve in the military since they won't have any *other* viable way of supporting themselves and their families.

- *"To provide for organizing, arming, and disciplining, the Militia, and for governing such Part of them as may be employed in the Service of the United States, reserving to the States respectively, the Appointment of the Officers, and the Authority of training the Militia according to the discipline prescribed by Congress;"*

CSC's Editorial Comment: Apparently, we've got the *"Defense"* thing dialed in. It's too bad we've messed up the *"general Welfare"* part of Article I … or the Republic wouldn't be at risk.

- *"To exercise exclusive Legislation in all Cases whatsoever, over such District (not exceeding ten Miles square) as may, by Cession of particular States, and the acceptance of Congress, become the Seat of the Government of the United States, and to exercise like Authority over all Places purchased by the Consent of the Legislature of the State in which *the Same shall be, for the Erection of Forts, Magazines, Arsenals, dock-Yards, and other needful Buildings;"*

 **CSC's Editorial Comment:** This must be working. We haven't had a State secede since 1861. Then again, the Federal government has just begun to *sue* States for trying to protect their citizens ... so, you just never know!

- *"And To make all Laws which shall be necessary and proper for carrying into Execution the foregoing Powers, and all other Powers vested by this Constitution in the Government of the United States, or in any Department or Officer thereof."*

 **CSC's Editorial Comment:** This is what I call the *"cesspool provision."* It's a catch-all that's used to justify Congress' entrance into a wide variety of issues that the Framers did not specifically enumerate. Notice that the Framers included *very restrictive* language to prevent Congress from wandering off course: the laws that Congress is empowered to make must be *"necessary"* and *"proper"* in executing the powers in this Section as well as throughout the *Constitution* and its related Amendments. Now, consider the laws that Congress routinely passes with all of their embedded pork. For example: bridges over non-existent rivers; gold-embossed playing cards for Air Force Two; a study of the effect of naval communications on a bull's potency; a study of the effect of Congress' *bull* on *our* potency (... okay, I just made up the last one, but the other examples are real). *"Necessary and proper?"* You decide!

Now, let's look at Article I, Section 8 in conjunction with the language of the Ninth and Tenth Amendments. The Ninth Amendment proclaims:

"The enumeration in the Constitution, of certain rights, shall not be construed to deny or disparage others retained by the people."

While the Tenth Amendment provides:

"The powers not delegated to the United States by the Constitution, nor prohibited by it to the States, are reserved to the States respectively, or to the people."

It seems like the Framers went out of their way to protect and preserve the rights of *the People* as well as the power of the States. Correspondingly, it seems logical to assume that they were *intentionally* trying to *limit* the scope of the Federal government (as they also did in Article I, Section 9); perhaps because with *size* comes *power* … and with *power* comes *abuse.* It's almost like the Framers were anticipating the challenge we would face in our efforts to retain the Republic and were trying to spell it out for us.

CSC's Platform Position: **All three Branches of our government need to revisit the *Constitution* … and remember, all those serving in Federal positions will be required to pass a Constitutional Test. The *Constitution* clearly *limits* the power it provides to the *Federal* government and is quite *expansive* in the power it reserves to the *States* under the Tenth Amendment. Perhaps even more telling are the *unenumerated* rights and privileges that are *retained* by *the People* under the Ninth Amendment.**

As a result, this Platform calls for our politicians to take the Framers at their word: that the *Federal* government should concentrate on the *"common Defense"* and those issues that impact the *"general Welfare"* of *"the United States."* It should stick to those powers that are *specifically* described in the *Constitution* and venture into other areas *only* if there is *clear* and *compelling* evidence that such issues impact the *"general Welfare"* of the country as a whole and that any related legislation is both *"necessary"* and *"proper."* There is no persuasive reason to add to our national debt by creating *new* agencies and regulations that add to the time and cost of doing business; nor is there any reason to add additional programs for which funding does not presently exist. Responsible leadership must work hard to *streamline* its operations rather than *expanding* them … and to *cut* costs rather than *add* to them.

If Congress would exercise this level of discipline, a balanced budget could be on the horizon in relative short order.

Given other recommendations in this Platform (such as single-issue legislation; legislative sponsorship; qualified civil servants with term limitations, etc.), there is every reason to believe that, once we have our spending under control and *real* leadership in place, we will be able to establish and maintain a *model* Republic that delivers upon the fiscal and social responsibilities anticipated by the Framers.

Before moving on, I feel compelled to comment upon a paradox that I see in today's political environment. Our candidates routinely ask us to *"trust"* them because *they* know what's best for us. Yet, they don't seem to trust *us*. We are treated as if we *need* their protection, when the reality is that the positions they seek *only* exist because *we* have chosen to delegate certain limited powers to them through the *Constitution*. The Framers didn't abdicate *any* of our individual freedoms in creating these positions. They merely fashioned a conduit through which we could *exercise* our freedoms more efficiently. So, this Platform calls for our political representatives to demonstrate their *"trust"* for *the People*. Don't try to build programs to protect us from ourselves. That's not your responsibility. Protect us from foreign and domestic aggression; protect us from the consequences of natural disasters; protect us from any *real* threat to our Republic ... but *please* stop trying to protect us from *ourselves*.

Benjamin Franklin said it best, *"The Constitution only gives people the right to pursue happiness. You have to catch it yourself."* It's not up to the Legislative Branch, the President, or the Supreme Court ... to bring their subjective interpretation of *"happiness"* into our lives. It's *their* job to *stay out of the way* so we can try to *"catch it"* for ourselves ... as *we* define it.

DEFENSE

Once again, Article I, Section 8 of the *Constitution* restricts Congress' power to raise and spend money to *two* issues that span the interests of *all* citizens: (1) *"the common Defense;"* and (2) the *"general Welfare"* ... *"of the United States."* So, let's start with Defense.

Federal Defense Responsibilities

In the big picture, a nation exists to defend its citizens against foreign and domestic threats. Foreign and domestic threats come in all shapes and sizes, so it is important to understand that the Federal government *only* should become involved when the *nature* of the threat crosses State lines, exceeds a State's capacity to adequately respond to the issue, or pertains to the entire country. Its involvement should only be expanded if the *general* welfare of the *Nation* would uniquely benefit from the contribution that a *"common"* or *"united"* effort would produce. In fact, for simplification purposes, let's always keep that in mind: there are issues for the *States* ... and there are issues for the *"United"* States. Hey, I'll bet that's where the name came from!

The term *"common Defense"* clearly applies to acts of aggression perpetrated against the United States (or one of its territories) by foreign entities. A great deal of the language in Article I, Section 8 is specific to military applications. However, *"common Defense"* may also be defined to include threats that create a risk to the *"general Welfare"* of *the People* of the United States that are *"necessary and proper"* for the Federal government to resolve ... whether those threats emanate from Man or Nature. For example: if the United States were to be attacked by a foreign country or terrorist organization, it would be the Federal government's obligation to defend its citizens because the threat would clearly be *"common"* to all citizens. It would also appropriate for the Federal government to become involved in defending us against threats which know no boundaries (such as pandemics, etc.) or that have been *specifically* prescribed in the *Constitution* (such as *"uniform Rules of Naturalization"* and the defense of our borders). And with respect to natural and man-made disasters (at least to the degree that such events can't *all* be blamed on the Bush Administration), the Federal government may be within its rights to intervene because the scale of such disasters may be beyond the capacity of the effected State (or States) to adequately address. In this regard, the Federal government serves as the ultimate *"insurance provider"* for the citizens of the United States. Since our politicians want to get into the insurance business anyway, this is an acknowledgment that the *"public option"* already exists ... except, in this case, it's not really an *option*. The Federal government is *obligated* to defend and provide humanitarian relief for its citizens in instances in which such assistance is *"necessary and proper;"* a burden which our government has *unselfishly* chosen to *extend* to the rest of the world ... and for which it receives *very* little gratitude.

In regard to the latter, about 20 percent of our annual Defense budget is spent providing humanitarian aid to *other* countries. Lest you think our Federal government has a monopoly on unconscionably bad decision-making, Non-Government Organizations (NGOs) that provide humanitarian relief often *refuse* funding and technology opportunities that evolve from within our military … because our military also *kills* people under certain circumstances (not very *"humanitarian"* of them … but sometimes a necessity within the context of their *primary* responsibility of *"waging peace"*). Of course, if you *polled* the Haitians who *lost* their *lives* or *limbs* in the last earthquake, and asked whether they really *cared* where the money or technology came from that could have *saved* their *lives* or *limbs* … I'm guessing that the vote would have come out in favor of the funding regardless of the source.

 **CSC's Platform Position:** **This Platform supports the traditional interpretation of the** *"common Defense"* **that the Federal government is to provide for** *"the United States"* **as described above.**

State Defense Responsibilities

In all such circumstances that a State can provide for the defense of its residents *without* the Federal government's assistance, it has the duty to do so. First responders, such as law enforcement officers, firefighters, and providers of humanitarian relief, all remain within the responsibility and jurisdiction of the State unless an associated issue crosses State lines or is of such a magnitude as to require Federal participation.

The same principle applies to the creation and enforcement of State laws. Unless an area of the law has been reserved to the Federal government, all other aspects of the law shall remain within the exclusive domain of the State unless the rights of another State are involved. For example: a State may resolve an issue of riparian rights with respect to a river that flows solely within that State; but Federal intervention might be required with respect to an issue of riparian rights with respect to a river that flows through or is otherwise shared by *more* than one State.

I'll address this in more detail when we explore the Tenth Amendment, which reserves a great deal of power to the States.

 **CSC's Platform Position:** If a State can defend its residents without the assistance of the Federal government, then States' authority shall prevail. However, if the citizens of multiple States are threatened ... or if a single State is overwhelmed by a disaster whose proportion exceeds the State's ability to adequately respond ... then Federal intervention would be both *"necessary and proper."* The Federal government is also *specifically* authorized to assess taxes to cover the cost of such assistance.

Because the Federal government is in a *unique* position to provide and fund such *"necessary and proper"* elements of *"common Defense"* that inure to the *"general Welfare"* of the citizens *"of the United States,"* this Platform wholly supports this *appropriate* application of Federal power as defined by the Framers.

The General Welfare

Beyond *"the common Defense,"* Article I, Section 8 extends the Legislative Branch's power to incur expenses and assume debt ... and extract sufficient funds to cover such expenses and debt through *"Taxes, Duties, Imposts and Excises"* ... to include instances in which the Federal government's intervention is both *"necessary and proper"* and serves as a benefit to the *"general Welfare of the United States."* Now, as we have discussed before, I think this language is pretty clear with respect to the hurdles that the Framers put in place to *prevent* runaway spending and any *abridgment* of any State or individual rights. I'm pretty sure that they didn't fight a war just to replace *one* Dictatorship with *another*.

Since the rest of the *National Platform of Common Sense* addresses issues that can be tied to the *"general Welfare of the United States,"* I'd like to take one more pass at examining the Framers' language because it is critically important to creating a Platform that is consistent with *protecting* and *preserving* the Republic. Once again, in relevant part, Article I, Section 8 states:

"The Congress shall have Power To lay and collect Taxes, Duties, Imposts and Excises to pay the Debts and provide for the common Defence (sic) and gen-

eral Welfare of the United States … (and) To make all Laws which shall be necessary and proper for carrying into Execution the foregoing Powers …"

- Other than with respect to *"the common Defense,"* the language of Article I, Section 8 basically gives power to Congress to *"make all Laws which shall be necessary and proper"* to *"provide for … the general Welfare of the United States."* Check!
- Webster's definition of *"necessary"* is *"absolutely needed."* Check!
- Webster's definition of *"proper"* is *"marked by suitability, rightness or appropriateness."* Check!
- Webster's definition of *"provide"* is *"to supply or make available."* Check!
- Webster's definition of *"general"* is *"involving, applicable to, or affecting the whole."* Check!
- Webster's definition of *"Welfare"* is *"aid in the form of money or necessities for those in need."* Check!

So, parsing this all together, we have: *"Congress shall have the power to enact laws … to supply or make available aid … in the form of money or necessities for those in need … in the instance that such need involves, is applicable to, or affects the <u>whole</u> United States; provided, however, that such need … is proven to be <u>absolutely</u> needed … and marked by suitability, rightness or appropriateness."* Got it!

That sounds like a pretty reasonable test to me. Otherwise, the power to govern shall be left to the States and neither the Federal nor State governments shall have the right to infringe upon the individual freedoms of *the People*. I shall adhere to that guidance in addressing all of the elements of *"general Welfare"* that remain. So without further adieu, let's take on the challenges of our time …

THE FIRST AMENDMENT: *FREEDOMS YOU CAN BELIEVE IN*

If you think that this Platform is only going to deal with the citizenship issue of *"illegal aliens,"* think again. While that's the *fashionable* element of citizenship upon which to take a stand today, it is *clearly* not the only one. In my opinion, far too many of us have come to take our citizenship for granted. We have become so enamored with *"causes"* and *"political correctness,"* we have ignored the signs of our Republic's erosion. We have entered into a *blended* form government of that was never intended by our Founding Fathers; a Republic in *form* and a Democracy in *appearance* that is drifting toward the tenets of Socialism (as Democracies inherently do). This is *exactly* the concern that Benjamin Franklin expressed when he proclaimed that we had established *"A Republic, if you can keep it."* Consider his words carefully: *"… if you can keep it."* Well, can we?

I think we can, but it will require a *new* level of responsibility associated with our citizenship. We need to recognize the signs of erosion from which our Republic is suffering and have the courage to *"exercise our rights."*

Due to a *gaping* abyss that has formed in our educational system, I fear that many of us are simply *intellectually blind* to the politics that appear before our very eyes. For some people, it's a matter of *elective blindness;* rejecting those things they *choose* not to see. But for most, it's a matter of *not recognizing* what is in plain sight. Politicians have become illusionists of the first order; an Ehrich Weiss who transforms into Harry Houdini when he takes the stage of politics. We are *mesmerized* by their promises and empowering thoughts … because we *want* to be. We may even *need* to be. So, we listen past their *"slight of word"* and become lost in the fantasy realms that they create. It isn't until the show is over and we *can't* get a *refund* for our *vote* … that we discover that the *trick* is on us. There's an old saying that's apropos: *"Fool me once, shame on you. Fool me twice, shame on me."*

So, let's look at some *"signs"* as Jeff Foxworthy might do it:
- When crosses (or other religious symbols), placed on government property in honor of fallen veterans, are ordered to be torn down even though the government clearly *isn't* attempting to *establish* a religious … *it might be a sign!*
- When children are not permitted to *freely exercise their religion* by praying in school … *it might be a sign!*
- When *freedom of speech* is dramatically undermined by the use of *"political correctness"* as an unjust form of social ostracism … *it might be a sign!*
- And when widely-diverse citizens *peacefully assemble to petition the government for a redress of grievances* and are called Nazi's and racists by the same people who endorse others who throw rocks, vandalize stores, and injure law enforcement officers and innocent bystanders at a protest (or *"peace"* rally) … *it might be a sign!*

We need to take our citizenship seriously and exercise our First Amendment rights, which states:

"Congress shall make no law respecting an establishment of religion, or prohibiting the free exercise thereof; or abridging the freedom of speech, or of the press; or the right of the people peaceably to assemble, and to petition the government for a redress of grievances."

Just because it was the *"first"* Amendment doesn't mean the Framers were *"just warming up."* In my opinion, it was the *First* Amendment because it defined our *most important* rights.

A former Senior Lecturer on Constitutional Law at the University of Chicago's Law School, who has since *elected* to change professions, has stated that:

"… the Constitution is a charter of <u>negative</u> liberties: [It] says what the states <u>can't</u> do to you, says what the federal government <u>can't</u> do to you, but it doesn't say what the federal government or the state government <u>must do</u> on your behalf."

Au contraire, mon ami! While I agree that the First Amendment *does* draw lines of demarcation relative to what the Federal government <u>cannot</u> do, it is within the context of what it *must do* on behalf of *each* of its citizens … in clear delineation of certain *"unalienable rights"* that are reserved to *the People* and protected from government usurpation.

Does anyone other than *me* have a problem with the obvious incongruities we have begun to passively accept over the past several decades? Does anyone else *care* that our basic rights are being diluted or eliminated altogether? Is this what the Framers had hoped for … or is it what they *feared?*

 **CSC's Platform Position:** The *National Platform of Common Sense* calls for the following … *"in Order to form a more perfect Union:"*

- *"Congress shall make no law … respecting an establishment of religion"*
   o The government *cannot* pick a religion as its own and try to force you to practice it.
- *"Congress shall make no law … prohibiting the free exercise of religion"*
   o The government *cannot* prohibit you from practicing the religion of your choice (or no religion at all) unless such practice poses an immediate and significant threat to property or person (*i.e.,* religious or non-religious zeal-

ots *cannot* try to *"cleanse the world"* of those with dissimilar beliefs through violent acts that threaten the safety or property of others).
- *"Congress shall make no law ... abridging the freedom of speech"*
  - You can say whatever you'd like to say *unless* it is *untrue* or is *intentionally* said to *incite* violence or *create* a reasonable fear of bodily harm.
- *"Congress shall make no law ... abridging the freedom of the press"*
  - The press may publish or broadcast whatever it chooses *unless* it either intentionally or irresponsibly *distorts* the truth or disseminates information that puts citizens' lives at risk (as it occasionally has by *"leaking"* national secrets, etc.)
  - Furthermore, the government shall neither fund nor in any other way influence or censor the press (*Pravda* is the alternative).
  - Should the press *"lose its way"* relative to its integrity or social mores and folkways, the public can impose its will upon the press quite effectively through economic sanctions. For example: if you believe the press is *abusing* its privileges, *stop reading* or *watching the offending press* and *stop buying any products and services from its sponsors*. You'll be *amazed* at how effective economic boycotts can be in a free market environment.
- *"Congress shall make no law ... abridging the right of the people peaceably to assemble"*
  - Would you like to get together as a group? Fine! Just don't start abusing the word *"peaceably."* Throw a rock; break a window; set a fire; vandalize a car; steal from a store; ignore the reasonable directives of law enforcement officers in their attempt to protect others; or threaten to harm others ... go directly to jail; do not pass *"Go!"* ... etc. If you have any doubt, look up the definition to the word *"peaceably."*
- *"Congress shall make no law ... abridging the right of the people to petition the government for a redress of grievances"*

- **Whether you call yourselves Democrats or Republicans, Libertarians, Tea Party Members, Green Party Members or a member any of the other dozens of Parties that exist ... or are just acting as an individual ... you have the *right* to petition the government if you disagree with it. And in a Republic, *your* voice has the chance to be heard. In *any* other form of government, you're probably just wasting your time. Monarchies and Theocracies have *no* interest in your complaints. Your thoughts are similarly *disinteresting* to Marxist, Communistic or Socialistic states in which the *"one party/one platform"* theme is pervasive. Even in a Democracy, if you're not in the majority ... well, good luck! So, thank the God of your choice (or just thank your *"lucky stars"*) that you live in a Republic.**

I know this sounds somewhat familiar. Okay, I admit it! I shamelessly *plagiarized* the First Amendment ... but it's *so* good, I couldn't think of a way to improve upon it other than to offer some clarification. The concepts only seem to give us problems when we try to *"spin"* them in a way that dramatically exceeds their original meaning. Sometimes, breaking things down into shorter phrases makes them easier to understand. I hope this exercise helps!

Before we leave this Section about the First Amendment, I feel that it is incumbent upon me to offend at least a *few* groups.

<u>Freedom of Religion</u>

To those atheists, who have enjoyed some degree of success in asserting that the First Amendment provides for *"separation of church and state"* ... to paraphrase a line from *Jerry McGuire*: *"Show me the language!"* What it *actually* says is:

"Congress shall make no law respecting an establishment of religion, or prohibiting the free exercise thereof ..."

So, unlike any of the forms of Dictatorships that we have already discussed (Monarchies, Theocracies, etc.), Congress cannot *proclaim* that a specific religious (or non-religious) belief be exclusively embraced by the citizens the United States (*i.e.*, it cannot endorse the Church of England as the *only* permitted religion of its people, which is the exact scenario from which many of the Pilgrims fled). Nor can Congress *"prohibit the free exercise thereof."* More specifically, Congress cannot *prevent* anyone from exercising their religious beliefs. So please, let's not pretend that a cross on *public* property is *offensive*, while the cross on the *private* property of church next door is *not*. If it really bothers you, just divert your eyes. Otherwise, who is to say that public buildings without some sort of religious symbol (*e.g.*, a cross, the Star of David, the angel Gabriel, a minaret, etc.) aren't equally disturbing to *"believers?"* Arguing in the alternative, should such buildings be torn down because *"believers"* are offended, and the *"naked"* buildings are an affront to their religious beliefs and *"prohibit their free exercise thereof."*

CSC's Platform Position: I'd like to see the ACLU (America's Crazy Lunatic Unit) either bring a lawsuit to force all government buildings to attach every religious symbol known to mankind (including a noticeably blank space to pay homage to atheists), or stop wasting everyone's time and money pandering to the *"squeaky wheel."* And that goes for Christmas trees, menorahs, crescents and stars, etc.

This Platform *endorses* posting *The Ten Commandments* on public property. What's the risk? People might stop *killing* each other, *stealing* from each other, *committing adultery* with each other, and begin *honoring* their mothers and fathers instead? I'm sorry! That just doesn't sound all that threatening to me.

Freedom of Speech

Then, there's *"Freedom of Speech:"*

"Congress shall make no law ... abridging the freedom of speech."

Other than the *"fighting words"* exception, which does not afford protection to statements that are made with the express intent to incite violence, and the exclusion for defamatory statements, I'm not sure we need to repress speech. It's funny ... or perhaps more accurately ... it's *disturbing* that our two major political Parties apparently see the need to either *limit* the speech of one another or to at least *defame* the integrity of the Opposition.

 **CSC's Platform Position:** This Platforms calls for all Americans, and *especially* our politicians, to follow the *"Four Way Test"* of the Rotary before we talk:

1. *Is it the TRUTH?*
2. *Is it FAIR to all concerned?*
3. *Will it build GOOD WILL and BETTER RELATIONSHIPS?*
4. *Will it be BENEFICIAL to all concerned?*

Can you imagine at how nice our lives would be if we followed this simple advice within the context of *Free Speech*? Otherwise, we're liable to find out that *Free Speech* isn't so "free."

Freedom of the Press

The First Amendment also protects the written word:
"Congress shall make no law … abridging … the freedom of the press."
As Thomas Jefferson said, "Our liberty cannot be guarded but by the freedom of the press, nor that be limited without danger of losing it." However, he recognized that integrity would be the key: "*Printing presses shall be subject to no other restraint than liableness to legal prosecution for false facts printed and published.*"
Of course, today, many of us feel that the once noble profession of reporting the news has given way to proselytizing one's own personal position; that the press has been bastardized, in a sense, into a media more fit for *entertainment* than *intellectual stimulation*. But alas, maybe times haven't changed all that much, as our good friend Thomas Jefferson said in 1807, *"Nothing can now be believed which is seen in a newspaper. Truth itself becomes suspicious by being put into that polluted vehicle. The real extent of this state of misinformation is known only to those who are in situations to confront facts within their knowledge with the lies of the day."*

 **CSC's Platform Position:** This Platform suggests that the pendulum needs to swing back to the time when the *news* media, in all of its forms, took more responsibility for its professionalism (*i.e.,* reporting *corroborated facts* rather than voicing jaded opinions from its bully pulpit).

Perhaps, Fox could stop proclaiming that its competitors aren't *"fair and balanced"* ... as if *all* of *its* programs *are;* perhaps CNN could return to its roots rather than pandering to its ratings; and perhaps MSNBC could tone down the *"tingling feeling"* that *"runs up the legs"* of its *blatantly* biased *"news"* team ... or at least buy them some Depend® for the *accidents* they must be having as they're overcome with excitement.

Conversely, this Platform *supports* the *nouveau-niche, social network "reporting"* of the intellectual giants whose stage names sound as if they've been educated in the hallways of Spanish Hotel. You've just got to admit ... *their* drivel makes the rest of us feel *much* better about ourselves!

In any event, I am all for a free ... and *professionally responsible* ... press.

Freedom to Assemble

As in any good Republic, the Framers made sure that *"We the People ..."* had a voice in our government. The First Amendment provides:

> *"Congress shall make no ... abridging ... the right of the people peaceably to assemble, and to petition the government for a redress of grievances."*

This seems particularly relevant today. I find the formation of the Tea Party to provide a great deal of entertainment; not because of *what* they do or *how* they do it, but because of how it is represented by the media (which is *why* I think the media has to rediscover its professional responsibility). As the Tea Party movement began to take shape, it was initially dismissed by the Democrats (as reported in the mainstream press) as being nothing more than a paid, political event staged by the Republicans. The Democrats should have *known* better! The Republicans haven't even *remotely* demonstrated the ability to organize anything *this* effective in years.

However, I can understand *why* the Democrats thought it was a Republican-organized and funded movement ... because the Democrats are used to populating and funding most of the more liberal rallies that we've seen on TV. It's the only type of *"movement"* they know. If they don't organize community workers and union employees, give them some free food and smokes, and bus them to the rally (or voting place), the crowd might be too small for even MSNBC to consider giving it any credence.

Those Tea Party people actually showed up *on their own!* They weren't organized by a Party ... but rather by a common ground. They saw our country beginning to spiral out of control and at least *cared* enough to look into the problem and express their dissatisfaction. Whether they will be successful in their endeavor remains to be seen, but they are the most *refreshing* demonstration of the right to *"peaceably ... assemble"* that this country has seen in quite some time.

And that raises another issue. How many times have you witnessed a *"peace rally"* where rocks were thrown, police were taunted, stores were vandalized, and cars were burned? Yet, they are portrayed as praiseworthy *"political demonstrations"* that are trying to address social grievances. On the other hand, Tea Parties of similar scale have been *comparatively* free of litter and conducted without incident (except for the few times some "outside" thugs have attended to stir things up). Given the stakes, the Tea Party's *"petitioning the government for a redress of grievances"* that include a visible erosion of our protected freedoms and a debt structure that cannot be sustained, versus groups clamoring for a cleaner environment, human rights, etc. (all laudable goals by the way, but a bit more amorphous and less threatening in the near-term to the very fabric of our society) ... you'd expect the *Tea-Baggers* to be the more vociferous and physically demonstrative of the two. Luckily, the mainstream press often *pretends* that they are.

CSC's Platform Position: This Platform endorses the right of citizens to present *all* such issues in an *orderly* and *law-abiding* manner ... with *respect* for the property and opinions of others. As citizens of the United States, it is our responsibility to stand up and say, "Hey, wait a minute..." if we believe that something is amiss. If you're *not* a citizen of the United States, go protest in your *own* country ... then, we'll visit you when you get out of jail.

This Platform would also like to see events reported with a *profound* respect for the *facts* and with an *equal enthusiasm* for the coverage given. Perhaps, maybe then, we could enjoy a positive change in our political and economic direction as well as begin to evolve the necessary reform needed in areas such as the environment and human rights.

This Platform also calls for a very *special* educational opportunity to be given to politicians who *irresponsibly denigrate* those citizens who are brave enough to stand up for what they believe in. Whether the citizens are passionate about global warming or our political frontier, they do *not* deserve to be dismissed as *"radicals"* or as members of an *"angry mob"* ... unless, in fact, they are. To those politicians who would jump to call such citizens Nazi's, Fascists, Socialists, Communists, etc. or bigots, racists, homophobes, etc., may you be sentenced to a course that forces you to better understand the meaning of those terms ... and then, may you be summarily voted out of office.

THE SECOND AMENDMENT: *Gun Control*

The Second Amendment provides:
"*A well regulated Militia, being necessary to the security of a free State, the right of the people to keep and bear Arms, shall not be infringed.*"

This one has a knack for polarizing people. As such, it's the perfect Amendment and issue to consider for an application of *common sense*.

CSC's Platform Position: This Platform has already endorsed the necessity of maintaining a *"well-regulated"* militia in the Section on Defense. It also supports *the Peoples'* right *"to keep and bear Arms."* However, this needs to be interpreted within a historical perspective.

Back in colonial times, the threat of any *"infringement"* of individual or States' rights by the Federal government *by force* was much greater. As a result, everyone was armed, and if necessary, *the People* could fight for their freedoms (individually or within the context of their State).

Think about it: in colonial times, it would have been musket-to-musket, pistol-to-pistol. Today, a confrontation between armed citizens and military troops would be standard and semi-automatic weapons (and perhaps a few illegal automatic weapons) versus Cruise missiles, Apache helicopters, F-22 Raptors, and maybe a small thermonuclear device or two. The military would be such a prohibitive favorite that Vegas wouldn't even take bets. We're talking the *Christians versus Lions* mismatch on steroids. Luckily, there is a very low probability that our Federal government would attempt a violent *coup* of any kind. It is *far* more likely that they would choose to "*slay a thousand citizens*" (or, at least, take away our freedoms) with a weapon better known to Hercules and the Philistines (*i.e.,* the jawbone of an ass).

So, you can continue to own a gun to protect your property against criminal invasions or threats, but *please* take classes on its safe use and storage (accidents *do* happen, and *children* are *notoriously* curious). If you use guns for hunting, please eat what you kill, and don't just hunt to mount a head as a trophy. If you do, everyone will just assume that it's to address some sort of *personal* inadequacy ... and you *don't* want *that* rumor to start making the rounds! That being said: hand guns, rifles and shotguns are okay; semi-automatic operation as well. That should provide a barrel of fun at the target range as well as allowing you to feel secure in your home and your person and to hunt anything that's legal. I think automatic weapons, hand grenades, bazookas, and surface-to-air missiles are a bit of an overkill (no pun intended); so please ... if you've been stockpiling them in the hills and have the need to play with them ... join the military.

THE THIRD AMENDMENT: *Military House Guests*

The Third Amendment doesn't get a lot of air time, and this won't be any exception. It states:
> "No Soldier shall, in time of peace be quartered in any house, without the consent of the Owner, nor in time of war, but in a manner to be prescribed by law."

I can't remember the last time the government asked me to house a soldier. I asked around, and nobody else had been asked either. So, we're just going to accept this and move on.

THE FOURTH AMENDMENT: *Personal Security*

It's time to talk about *personal* security ... not in the sense of the *Second Amendment* and physical security ... but rather in terms of the *Fourth Amendment* that provides:
> "The right of the people to be secure in their persons, houses, papers, and effects, against unreasonable searches and seizures, shall not be violated, and no Warrants shall issue, but upon probable cause, supported by Oath or affirmation, and particularly describing the place to be searched, and the persons or things to be seized."

Thanks to the ACLU (America's Crazy Lunatic Unit) and the progressive expansion of these rights to *"all things living and dead,"* the pendulum may have swung too far with respect to protecting the government from infringing upon this area. We now extend Miranda Rights to *terrorists* for fear of being viewed as *"politically incorrect"* by the rest of the world or, perhaps, even offending the terrorists who remain at large.

If we're going to expand these protections, I'd rather see the expansion be in the form of legislation that limits invasions into our personal lives by unsolicited Internet SPAM, junk mail, and telemarketing. Maybe we wouldn't have bandwidth issues relative to the web or our telecommunications systems, and the United States Postal Service would be able to process snail-mail more expeditiously, if all the Consumer-Related Advertising Programs (*CRAP* for short) were removed from our lives. Our personal information is *"seized"* all the time and used in an effort to exploit us. All you progressives out there who need a new cause ... how about taking up *this* one ... or do you use these same methods to champion too many of *your* programs to risk losing them as a tool?

 **CSC's Platform Position:** *The People* shall remain *"secure in their persons, houses, papers, and effects, against unreasonable searches and seizures."*

Even though studies show that no one really understands the implication of receiving their Miranda Rights, this Platform is okay with providing the warning.

However, this Platform *rejects* the need to give such warning (or rights) to *terrorists*. If someone tries to crash a plane, blow up a building, or shoot a bunch of innocent people, this Platform doesn't harbor a lot of concern for such individual's rights. In fact, this Platform believes the terrorist act itself shall serve as a *"request to suspend"* such rights.

And speaking of *"platforms," common sense* suggests that *platforms* and ... oh, I don't know ... maybe *water*... may be used together to *gather information* that might *prevent* additional attempts to *kill* Americans and other innocent people from occurring. Now, before all you bleeding hearts out there get angry and assume that I'm endorsing *water boarding* ... I'm *not*. Let me be clear ... (hey, that sounds *so* Presidential) ... I am *against* water boarding. Instead, I think that terrorist should be questioned *politely*. If they refuse to answer, we should be permitted to smack them over the head with a platform or board of some type. Then, we could splash some water on them to revive them so we could ask them *politely* again ... and again ... and again ... until such time that we have the information we need to protect innocent lives. See! And to think that *some* of you probably jumped to the conclusion that I supported water boarding.

As an aside: I do find it interesting that we've committed to closing down Guantanamo because the mere *existence* of the facility *incites* terrorists ... but we're *okay* with having our Attorney General, when talking about the potential capture of Osama Bin Laden, state: *"Either he will be killed by us, or he will be killed by his own people so that he is not captured by us. We know that. ... (We'll be) reading Miranda rights to his corpse, because I think that's what we're going to be dealing with. He is not going to be alive."* I'm sure that the discerning members of al-Qaeda will distinguish between the two. They will *undoubtedly* look at Guantanamo as a symbol of American Imperialism and will merely dismiss Eric Holder's comments as the ramblings of some political buffoon. I know that I have!

Now, for those law aficionados out there ... we ought to rethink the *"fruits of the poisoned tree"* doctrine within the context of *common sense*. In other words, we need to stop dismissing criminal cases because the evidence that was gathered wasn't specific to the original probable cause for which the suspect was stopped or for which a warrant was issued.

To put this into perspective, cases are thrown out of court every day based upon technical deficiencies tied to the gathering of evidence. If someone is stopped (or a warrant is issued) for stealing an acetone-based nail product from a women's cosmetics store, and during the subsequent search, massive amounts of bomb-making elements are found ... or drugs that could be sold to fund a terrorist enterprise ... the defendant might get to *"walk free"* because the evidence was unrelated to the initial search. *This* Platform calls for a legislative correction of this issue so that terrorist, murderers, rapists, pedophiles, etc. *cannot* leave courtrooms with smiles on their faces because something was *fairly* discovered during the course of investigating another crime for which there was probable cause to suspect them. Such legislation can certainly be framed in such a way that the evidence must be compelling, related to a first degree felony, and acquired pursuant to an otherwise legal search to protect against its abuse; but criminals should *not* be allowed to escape a *common sense* application of the law that is designed to protect the lives and property of *innocent* citizens.

As for unsolicited SPAM, telemarketing, and junk mail initiatives that waste time, money and resources, generally annoy the recipient, and can lead to civil and criminal abuse: just *stop* it! Remember our discussion of the Golden Rule? If you don't like it when it happens to you, don't do it to others. Otherwise, this Platform calls for legislation that clearly addresses *this* invasion of privacy and puts an end to it.

THE FIFTH AMENDMENT: *The Forgotten Freedoms*

"Taking the Fifth" is not the equivalent of complying with a B.Y.O.B. invitation. The Fifth Amendment provides:

"No person shall be held to answer for a capital, or otherwise infamous crime, unless on a presentment or indictment of a Grand Jury, except in cases arising in the land or naval forces, or in the Militia, when in actual service in time of War or public danger; nor shall any person be subject for the same offense to be twice put in jeopardy of life or limb; nor shall be compelled in any criminal case to be a witness against himself, nor be deprived of life, liberty, or property, without due process of law; nor shall private property be taken for public use, without just compensation."

It obviously covers a lot of territory relative to the *"general Welfare"* of this country's citizens. So, let's get right to the Platform impact.

CSC's Platform Position: As for the *"no person shall answer for a capital, or otherwise infamous crime unless on a presentment or indictment of a Grand Jury,"* I think we do a pretty good job of complying until we start drifting away from the *exception*. Specifically, *"except in cases arising in the land or naval forces, or in the Militia, when in actual service in time of War or public danger."* In particular, *"in time of ... public danger"* would seem to apply to the terrorist threats we have suffered since September 11th, 2001. This just reaffirms this Platform's position that terrorist suspects are *not* necessarily entitled to the protections otherwise afforded by our criminal justice system. The risk is simply *too* great to ignore the realities associated with it. The Framers weren't particularly well known for their leniency toward treasonous activity, and I rather doubt that they would have lost a lot of sleep over reserving a different form of justice for terrorist suspects than they reserved for citizens in general.

While an occasional injustice might occur because of the *"Double Jeopardy"* provision (*i.e., "nor shall any person be subject for the same offense to be twice put in jeopardy of life or limb"*), this Platform sees no compelling need to change that provision. Prosecutors should take their best shot when they have it, and no one should be required to spend their remaining years constantly defending against the *same* charge. Beside, those who luckily escape conviction the first time are likely to *"mess up"* at a later date trying to recover their personal property in a Vegas hotel room ... at gunpoint. As a good friend of mine used to say, *"Time wounds all heels!"*

Which brings us to some of the more interesting elements of the Fifth Amendment:

- A person shall not be *"compelled in any criminal case to be a witness against himself."*
    - While this might occasionally prevent us from being entertained by a chain of expletives should a Chicago politician ever refuse to take the stand in his or her defense, it's probably a *"good call."* It would be like asking you to tie the knot on your noose before they hang you ... it *just* isn't right. Sometimes a Defendant's testimony really *isn't* required if the Prosecution hasn't made its case. On other occasions, despite being charged to ignore it, members of the jury tend to apply *common sense* ... whether they ever admit it; so it all works out in the end.
- A person shall not be *"deprived of life, liberty, or property, without due process of law"*
    - Unfortunately, this one happens more often than we care to admit. Under the Fifth Amendment, *"due process"* only applies to the Federal government, but through the Fourteenth Amendment, it essentially also applies to the States. Generally speaking, you're supposed to get adequate notification and a hearing with a neutral judge. This concept gets routinely trampled in the *real* world unless someone draws a line in the sand and forces the issue. Our Federal government *can't* even get this right in the controlled environment of Congress. Consider the 24 hour notice given to vote on amendments to the 2,700+ page Health Care Reform Bill. Can even the most zealous of proponents suggest that *this* is sufficient notice? And while the Fifth

Amendment isn't directly applicable to the example, I think the example's disregard for what is *right* is blatant enough to show how extreme the problem has become ... and we're not even going to go into issue of whether any resultant *"hearings"* are *truly* held before *"neutral judges."*

- o Therefore, the *National Platform of Common Sense* declares that *"due process"* needs to be applied *as intended* and not just restricted to more visible criminal cases. *"Notice"* needs to be provided on a *common sense* basis (meaning: sufficiently in advance) to all effected parties for issues that potentially impact *"life, liberty, or property;"* and all associated hearings need to be presided over by an *experienced* and *impartial* trier of fact.

- A person shall not have their *"private property ... taken for public use, without just compensation."*
    - o The RNC Platform mentioned the *Kelo* decision. In *Kelo v. City of New London*, 545 U.S. 469 (2005), the Supreme Court extended the right of eminent domain to take a private residence for the purpose of private development as long as the private development has a *"legitimate ... public purpose"* rather than the traditional limitation of requiring the taking to be for a *clear "public use."* This *should* raise concern because it clearly extends the governments right to take your property for an *intangible "public purpose,"* which may never occur (as was the case in *Kelo*) ... as opposed to limiting such right to circumstances involving a tangible *"public use."*
    - o But then, why pay *anything* for your property? Why *distinguish* it from your personal income? After all, it's just a *tangible* manifestation of how you have elected to *use* your income. If we allow our politicians to believe they have the power to *"redistribute the wealth,"* why not just allow them to *"redistribute the property"* as well? Let's see ... you're house is bigger than mine. I'll *take* it! Your car is newer than mine. I'll take *that* too! And I really like your watch ...

- This Platform calls for an *enforcement* of the Fifth Amendment; particularly with regard to:
  - Distinguishing between the rights of *citizens* and those who *threaten* our safety during *"time of War or public danger"* and clarifying that *"public danger"* incorporates *any* time and *any* attack by a terrorist.
  - Mandating *"due process"* in the form of the *"transparency"* in policy formulation and execution (as has been *promised* but *not* delivered), with adequate notice from a *common sense* perspective to allow an informed review and response by the parties involved and the promise that, if disagreement shall exist, an open and fair debate shall be held before (and decided by) an experienced and impartial trier of fact.
  - Enforcing the importance of *all* property rights, which shall apply *not only* to *real property*, but to *personal property* as well (*including* personal income and savings) ... to prevent an unjust taking by the government, an unjust enrichment of the government, and a destruction of the opportunity to secure one's own version of the *"American Dream"* through hard work and persistence.

THE SIXTH AMENDMENT: *Fast, Public and Impartial*

The Sixth Amendment is not: *"I see dead people."* That's *The Sixth Sense!* The Sixth Amendment states:

> *"In all criminal prosecutions, the accused shall enjoy the right to a speedy and public trial, by an impartial jury of the State and district wherein the crime shall have been committed, which district shall have been previously ascertained by law, and to be informed of the nature and cause of the accusation; to be confronted with the witnesses against him; to have compulsory process for obtaining witnesses in his favor, and to have the Assistance of Counsel for his defence (sic)."*

Breaking it into smaller parts ... if you're accused of a crime, you're entitled to:

- A Speedy Trial
- A Public Trial

- An Impartial Jury within the State and district where you are accused of having committed the crime
- Being informed of what you're being charged with having done
- Confronting those who testify against you
- Compelling favorable witnesses appear to testify on your behalf, and
- Having an attorney represent you or help you with your defense.

These seem pretty good to me.

 **CSC's Platform Position:** This Platform calls for *adherence* to the Sixth Amendment as it stands. Unfortunately, that's not *always* the case. For example:

- **A Speedy Trial … doesn't *always* occur.**
    - Khalid Sheikh Mohammed was captured on March 1, 2003. Our Attorney General has decided that he should be entitled to the full rights of our citizens including a trial in a Federal court rather than before a Military Tribunal. Despite being entitled to a *"speedy trial"* based upon the Attorney General's generosity, this media bonanza still hasn't established a venue, much less a trial date. If this is an example of a *"speedy trial,"* I'm unimpressed. However, given that the defendant has admitted to having masterminded the terrorist attacks of 9/11, I'm okay with him being locked away for a *long* time before he's brought to justice (a scenario that would actually be *permitted* within the context of his prior status as an *"enemy combatant"*).

Just as an aside: I sure hope that a motion for mistrial is never filed based upon this delay; and if there is, I hope it's not granted. But we can all thank Attorney General Holder for creating the possibility.

    - This Platform calls for the *"speedy trial"* provision of the Sixth Amendment to be enforced in traditional criminal scenarios … and for enemy combatants to be tried in Military Tribunals.
- **A Public Trial**
    - Unfortunately, the press may have taken this provision too *literally*. A *"public trial"* means that the trial can not be held in secret; allowing people to be locked away

without anyone ever knowing. It *doesn't* mean having the press try the accused in the media *before* the case is even called ... or in some cases, before the accused is even *arrested*.
- This Platform calls for the *press* to exercise some discretion when it comes to ruining a potentially innocent individual's life. Sure, it sells advertising and gains readers and viewers, but the court system seems better equipped to actually conduct a *fair* and *impartial* hearing. I'm not restricting the press from exercising its freedom. I'm just asking members of the press to pretend the story is being written about *them* instead of someone else ... and assuming, for the sake of argument, that the accused is *"innocent until proven guilty."* Just leave it to the *judges* to preside over the facts and law so that the *jury* can deliberate in as *meaningful* and *unbiased* a way as possible. *Then*, report on the *outcome* to your heart's content *after* the verdict is rendered.

- An Impartial Jury within the State and district where you are accused of having committed the crime
  - Due to the pre-trial media frenzy that's created by newsworthy criminal cases, it's tough to assemble an *"impartial jury of the State and district wherein the crime shall have been committed."* The cooperation of the press (as was previously called for) would go a long way toward assuring that justice is done in this regard.
- Being informed of what you're being charged with having done
  - I always thought the Framers should have moved this to the *top* of the list. It seems that it would be a good starting point to know what the charges are. That being said, its placement is irrelevant as long as it's enforced.
- Confronting those who testify against you
  - This is a good idea that is generally honored.
- Compelling favorable witnesses appear to testify on your behalf, and
  - As with the previous element, this is a good idea that is generally honored.

- Having an attorney represent you or help you with your defense.
  - This is incorporated in one's Miranda Rights. We've all watched enough television to know that *"You have a right to an attorney. If you cannot afford one, one will be appointed for you by a court of law."* Admittedly, it may be a grossly over-worked Public Defender who's appointed to your case, so you may not get the personal legal attention of a Bernie Madoff or O.J. Simpson ... but you *are* entitled to *"Assistance of Counsel."* This, again, is a good idea that this Platform believes should continue to be enforced.

THE SEVENTH AMENDMENT: *An Example of Inflation*

The Seventh Amendment provides:
> *"In Suits at common law, where the value in controversy shall exceed twenty dollars, the right of trial by jury shall be preserved, and no fact tried by a jury, shall be otherwise re-examined in any Court of the United States, than according to the rules of the common law."*

This area of individual rights is pretty firmly established. However, if the language were ever to be adjusted for inflation, the dollar amount would probably be a lot more than $20.

THE EIGHTH AMENDMENT: *Nothing in Excess*

The Eighth Amendment states:
> *"Excessive bail shall not be required, nor excessive fines imposed, nor cruel and unusual punishments inflicted."*

Since *"excessive"* is not defined, this leaves a lot of room for interpretation. Hopefully, it is always interpreted with *common sense*.

CSC's Platform Position: This Platform calls for the punishment to fit the crime ... and that goes for bail as well. Our courts already consider the nature and circumstances of the offense and the Defendant's past criminal history, flight risk, financial resources, etc., when setting bail. This Platform suggests imposition of what I call *The Madoff Memorial Provision*, which states:

"In a crime of embezzlement, bail shall be set at ten times the amount believed to have been embezzled."

Since bail bonds usually require ten percent down, if the accused comes up with bail, you know that he or she probably did the crime. Then, all you have to do is *"nationalize"* the bail bond industry ... or create what I like to call *"the public option"* ... with respect to embezzlement cases. If the government is holding the bail payment, all it has to do is convict the accused and then *redistribute* the bail proceeds to the victims. Problem solved! No more long and unsuccessful audits and investigations. The government gets its conviction and the victims are *"made whole."*

With respect to *"excessive fines,"* we now know that the Executive Branch can *"negotiate"* at least $20 billion (as in the case of British Petroleum and the Gulf oil spill). Who knows what the upper limit might be? We didn't even need to *go* to *court* to get that amount. We only had to practice Chicago politics from the White House. I'm sure everything was on the *"up-and-up"* or we would have already *apologized* to the world for our arrogance.

Now, my personal favorite among Amendment debates is the application of the phrase *"cruel and unusual"* as a limitation on *"punishment."* I believe that *common sense* dictates that two facts be taken into account: (1) the Framers consciously chose to use the conjunction *"and"* rather than *"or"* to join the words *"cruel AND unusual"*; and (2) during colonial times, they still had firing squads, public hangings, and other punishments that many would considered to be *"cruel"* in today's society. Again, I think this gives us a lot of latitude when it comes to what's constitutes *"cruel AND unusual punishment."* This Platform suggests that it's probably okay to exact *really "cruel"* punishments ... as long as we do it consistently so it can't be deemed to be *"unusual."* I'll discuss this in more detail later when I address how to handle terrorists.

THE NINTH AMENDMENT: *Power to the People!*

The Ninth Amendment is incredibly important to *the People*. It states:
> "The enumeration in the Constitution, of certain rights, shall not be construed to deny or disparage others retained by the people."

CSC's Platform Position: This is too elegant a statement with which to tamper. Instead, this Platform merely endorses it *without limitation*. It means that the Framers believed that, *when in doubt*, the *power* should reside in *the People* ... *not* in the State, and *certainly not* in the Federal government. Now, ask yourself: *"When was the last time you felt more empowered than the government?"* It's time to get back to the basics!

THE TENTH AMENDMENT: *State Your Case*

The Tenth Amendment ties up the loose ends between the Federal government, the State governments, and *the People* (in conjunction with the *Ninth Amendment*) and provides:
> "The powers not delegated to the United States by the Constitution, nor prohibited by it to the States, are reserved to the States respectively, or to the people."

CSC's Platform Position: Again, the language is simple, to the point, and endorsed without reservation by this Platform. If the power isn't *expressed* within the *Constitution*, the Federal government does *not* have the power. Such power either resides within the State or is reserved to *the People*. It is impossible to articulate it more eloquently than that.

The Framers established a pecking order: limited power (although grand in *scale*) resides within the Federal government; more *expansive* power resides within the States, limited by their sphere of geographic authority; and *the remainder of the power* shall remain with *the People*. If you need more proof, look to the *Preamble* to the *Constitution:*

"We the People of the United States, in Order to form a more perfect Union, establish Justice, insure domestic Tranquility, provide for the common defence (sic), promote the general Welfare, and secure the Blessings of Liberty to ourselves and our Posterity, do ordain and establish this Constitution for the United States of America." Again, let's break it down:
- Who? ... "We the People of the United States"...
- For what purpose? ... "in Order to:
    - *Form a more perfect Union,*
    - *Establish Justice*
    - *Insure domestic Tranquility,*
    - *Provide for the common defence (sic),*
    - *Promote the general Welfare, and*
    - *Secure the Blessings of Liberty "* ...
- For whom? ... "To ourselves and our Posterity" ...
- Do what? ... "Do ordain and establish this Constitution for the United States of America."

Please note that it is *the People* who created the *Constitution* for *themselves* and for their *future* generations. *The People* set the rules, and they did so to *protect* and *preserve* their *own* rights and freedoms; the rights and freedoms they fought to *secure* from the British Monarchy.

Now, couple that with the *Declaration of Independence* that launched this movement, which states in part:

"We hold these truths to be self-evident, that all men are created equal, that they are endowed by their Creator with certain unalienable Rights, that among these are Life, Liberty and the pursuit of Happiness.--That to secure these rights, Governments are instituted among Men, deriving their just powers from the consent of the governed, --That whenever any Form of Government becomes destructive of these ends, it is the Right of the People to alter or to abolish it, and to institute new Government, laying its foundation on such principles and organizing its powers in such form, as to them shall seem most likely to effect their Safety and Happiness. Prudence, indeed, will dictate that Governments long established should not be changed for light and transient causes; and accordingly all experience hath shewn, that

mankind are more disposed to suffer, while evils are sufferable, than to right themselves by abolishing the forms to which they are accustomed. But when a long train of abuses and usurpations, pursuing invariably the same Object evinces a design to reduce them under absolute Despotism, it is their right, it is their duty, to throw off such Government, and to provide new Guards for their future security." Once again, breaking these words down for clarity, we have:
- *"We hold these truths to be self-evident,*
- *That all men are created equal,*
- *That they are endowed by their Creator with certain unalienable Rights,*
- *That among these are Life, Liberty and the pursuit of Happiness."*

Notice that these *"unalienable rights"* only pertain to *the People* rather than the government, which will become even more evident as we continue:
- *"That to secure these rights, Governments are instituted among Men*
- *Deriving their just powers from the consent of the governed"*

This ideal, upon which the *Constitution* is based, provides that the *government* is created to *serve the People* with *their* consent. (... Continuing ...)
- *"That whenever any Form of Government becomes destructive of these ends,*
- *It is the Right of the People to alter or to abolish it,*
- *And to institute new Government,*
- *Laying its foundation on such principles and organizing its powers in such form, as to them shall seem most likely to effect their Safety and Happiness."*

The Framers were to form a new government that would be organized in such as way as to create and preserve the highest probability of securing *"Safety and Happiness"* ... again, for *the People*. . (... Continuing ...)
- *"Prudence, indeed, will dictate that Governments long established should not be changed for light and transient causes;*

- *And accordingly all experience hath shewn, that mankind are more disposed to suffer, while evils are sufferable, than to right themselves by abolishing the forms to which they are accustomed.*
- *But when a long train of abuses and usurpations, pursuing invariably the same Object evinces a design to reduce them under absolute Despotism,*
- *It is their right, it is their duty, to throw off such Government, and to provide new Guards for their future security."*

This is an acknowledgement that breaking away from an existing form of government is not an *easy* decision *nor* should it be. But there comes a time when the accumulation of a government's appropriation and abuse of power threatens the elimination of personal freedoms in favor of tyrannical rule ... and at that time, it becomes *the People's* right and *duty* to *change* leadership.

Clearly, the Framers intended to create a government that *served the People* rather than one in which *the People* served the government. At the Federal level, the government should be focused on *"the big picture"* (*i.e.,* establishing *"Justice,"* insuring *"domestic Tranquility,"* and providing for the *"Defense and general Welfare"*). Since the States are closer to *the People*, they are expected to facilitate more specific functions that are directed at *serving the People* so that they may enjoy the *"Blessings of Liberty."*

Compare that to where we are today. Do you feel like *you* serve the government or that the *government* serves you? If you feel like *you* serve the government, then you have the *right* ... and the *duty* ... to do something about it. That's what elections are for. *Cast your vote* to *change* leadership. Conversely, if you feel like the *government* serves *you*, then that's what elections are for. *Cast your vote* to *preserve* the *status quo*. It's not complicated. Either way: study the candidates; go to the polls; and cast an *informed* vote. Otherwise, please stay home! Let those who *care* enough about this country to take the time to fully understand the issues and the positions of the candidates make the decision on your behalf. In my opinion, that's a

much better alternative for our country than going to the polls to cast your vote based solely on Party affiliation, name familiarity, or because someone provided the transportation and offered you some cigarettes or a meal if you'd vote the way they *told* you to. The Republic and our freedoms are too precious to be left in the hands of those who do not care.

Now that we've explored some of the issues that arise as a result of the Bill of Rights, let's move on to the contemporary issues of our times.

THE ECONOMY

Since we've buried ourselves in debt over the last few years, I thought it might be appropriate to start with an examination of Economic Reform. The first Clinton Presidential campaign had it right: *"It's the economy, stupid."* Congress can waste a lot of time and money passing social legislation that attracts votes and more deeply entrenches stereotypes, or it can do what it is actually *authorized* to do: concentrate on providing a *"common Defense"* and implement programs that are *"necessary and proper"* to accommodate the *"general Welfare of the United States."* Asking our current gang in Washington, D.C. to solve our economic problems is a little like asking Heidi Montag to serve as a spokesperson for natural beauty. The two just don't seem to go together any more.

Our current President is quick to condemn *"big business"* and announce that the *government* needs to *take control* to protect our interests. That is to be expected. He is a Democrat, and his Party has a *vested* interest in maintaining a *"We vs. They"* dynamic between *"big business"* and the rest of us. It allows his Party to place the vast majority of us within the single biggest *"oppressed minority"* category in existence ... outside of the *"Richest 5 Percent vs. The Rest of Us"* category (and the two are so similar). Remember my earlier discussion about *Envy?* We just can't help ourselves as human beings!

As I've mentioned before, this is a classic application of the *Robin Hood* strategy. Big business is the Sheriff of Nottingham, and the Democrat-led government is Robin Hood. It's important that we *believe* that our best interests are *only* served by a Democrat-led government ... so that *they* can maintain political control. In that regard, the Democratic Party has done an *outstanding* job of aligning the Republican Party with *"big business,"* and the Republican Party is too strategically *inept* to know how to combat this pretense.

The deductive reasoning is as follows: *"big business"* is greedy and a threat to *your* best interests; Republicans support *"big business;"* therefore, Republicans are greedy and a threat to *your* best interests – vote for Democrats. Besides, *"big business"* and the *"rich"* are almost one and the same, and you know how much you *envy* the rich! It's just not *fair* that they have more than you! Mr. Hood, please *"redistribute the wealth."*

This must be working because the Democrats are in power. And to hold it, they'll have to deliver a little *"redistribution"* or we won't be *"feeling the love."* Their *modus operandi* is to do this is through *"reform,"* even though the *Oath of Office* requires the Federal officials to *"preserve, protect and defend the Constitution of the United States"* ... not *ignore* it. And we've already got a number of examples of *"reform"* on the table. There's the Stimulus Bill, Health Care Reform Bill, and most recently the Wall Street Reform Bill. The government *is* taking charge!

Of course, that's not necessarily a *good* thing. It flies in the face of the Republic that the Framers were trying to create. Try to imagine the horror Washington, Jefferson and Madison would be experiencing if they were alive today to see what has transpired. In the infamous Stimulus Bill, our government *ordained* itself with the right to decide who's *"too big to fail."* Since then, it's essentially *nationalized* the American automobile industry (*sans* Ford); trampling the rights of secured creditors in the process, ignoring well-formed bankruptcy law, and turning a disproportionate share of ownership over to the United Auto Workers union (to which the Party in power is *deeply* beholden from a political perspective).

With respect to Health Care Reform, the most troublesome issue was abortion. Oh, not *that* kind of *abortion!* I'm talking about *"abortion"* in the colloquial sense, which Dictionary.com defines as *"a shambles; mess; anything that fails to develop, progress, or mature, as a design or project."* That pretty much sums it up: 2,700 pages of untested and disjointed theories that risk gutting *one-sixth* of our Nation's economy.

Then, there's Wall Street Reform. It was destined to pass ... well, because it was named *"Wall Street Reform"* ... which is almost synonymous with all that is evil. Now, we can rest in the comfort that our *"Regulators"* will be ... well, *regulating!* We're not exactly sure *what* ... or *how* ... but we're sure they'll be regulating *something*. Note: these are essentially the *same* Regulators who were in place while the economic meltdown occurred; except now we've given them even *more* power to use ineffectively. I can only imaging how proud the Framers would be. Why, we've *almost* recreated a Monarchy!

Of course, all of these new bills will require the creation of a *ton* of new agencies. Well, they won't really *require* them ... but that's how business is done in Washington, D.C. these days. Health Care Reform alone brought us 159 *new* agencies. The *really* great news is that each of these agencies will spend the next few *decades* promulgating regulations that will further intrude upon our freedoms. They'll also spend a great deal of time *marking their territories* to justify their ongoing existence. On the plus side, they'll expand exponentially over time; creating a whole new raft of jobs for the *"bureaupaths"* of the future (my term for *pathological* bureaucrats). Maybe that's the current Administration's *"secret plan"* to reduce unemployment.

A good friend of mine once told me about a term they used to use in the military during Vietnam: *"NUGs"* ... which stood for *"New Useless Guys."* Nothing generates *NUGs* like government expansion, and *that* translates into money. Lots of it! You see, we have to *pay* for all these new agencies and their *NUGs,* for the *regulations* they will create over time, for the *oversight* groups that will need to be put into place, and for the enforcement of the regulations that will infringe on our rights. Repeat after me: *"The floggings will continue until morale improves."*

CSC's Platform Position: Plugging the leak in government spending, which makes BP's problem in the Gulf of Mexico look somewhat trivial, should help considerably when it comes to righting our country's economic ship. Contrary to the problem in the Gulf, *eliminating "skimmers"* is just what the doctor ordered; those pork-ladened earmarks that get attached to our Nation's business to buy a vote here, curry favor there, and generally pay off political debts. The *"single issue"* approach to legislation and the associated accountability will go a long way toward correcting this weakness.

Instead of frivolously creating *new* agencies, we need to *consolidate* those that we *already* have to gain operating efficiencies and concentrate power accordingly. Do we really *need* 159 new Health Care agencies in addition to the dozens that already exist to affect change? I think not. Health Care

Reform *can* be cured! Again, the *"single issue"* approach would clarify where bipartisan support actually exists as opposed to the *"here it is, take it or leave it"* approach that was proffered in cramming through the current Health Care Reform Bill. I think you'd be surprised at how much agreement there would be on the truly *critical* issues. Then, the Republicans wouldn't have to be painted as the Party of *"No"* ... and the Democrats wouldn't have to appear to be the Party of *"Don't Know!"*

Once we get a higher-caliber of talent in Washington, a lot of these problems will go away. But in the interim, I think we're going to have to *"connect the dots"* for our current politicians. In that regard, this Platform calls for the following:

- An assessment and elimination of *all* unnecessary redundancy in our Federal government (and no, I don't think we need 213 new agencies to complete this exercise).
    - Agencies will be consolidated whenever possible. It's like resolving fractions to their least common denominator (don't worry ... I'll be addressing our educational system as well).
    - The reduction study shall include an assessment of the rules that govern the number of members that serve within the House of Representatives. The ratio of Congressmen has been historically based upon population density. There has been no adjustment for the vast improvements in transportation and communication that have evolved over the years. Coupled with my previous proposals to change to a *single-term system* and an elimination of the *ridiculous* campaign rituals that waste time and money, we should be able to achieve *huge* productivity gains. Think of how efficient our government would be if our legislators and President spent their time doing their *jobs* rather than running for re-election or supporting the campaigns of *other* Party members. If this becomes the case, we should be able to *reduce* the number of Congressman while *improving* the representation we receive. We can redirect the associated savings to offset the compensation increase this Platform called for earlier to

attract higher quality candidates. You want *"Change?"* I'll give you *"Change!"*
- A limited number of small (and I *do* mean *small*), *non-partisan* committees comprised of the *best experts* we can find will be *"on call"* to help identify problems, assess alternatives, and provide recommendations relative to the framing of *"single issue"* legislation. Our present practice of entrusting the future of our country to inexperienced, and in some cases, not particularly well-informed politicians is *dangerous* at best. The *Declaration of Independence*, the *Constitution*, and the *Bill of Rights* were not left to the drafting of novices. In today's world, we can be no less diligent.
- Government officials will be precluded from ignoring well-formed law (such as Bankruptcy Law) without open debate and the passage of associated legislation. Just as the Bush Administration was *properly* criticized for the Patriot Act's infringement upon certain fundamental rights, so should the Obama Administration be castigated for its abrogation of certain principles of freedom that are otherwise deeply woven into the fabric of our country.
  - Rather than *nationalizing* an industry or imposing its ideologies through *"Cap and Trade"* and similarly veiled efforts to arrest control over a given market, our government shall be *restrained* from exercising its influence through inequitable punishments (*i.e.,* taxes, fines, etc.) and, instead, shall focus on *proactively supporting* new initiatives in a way that will accelerate their development.

As an example, private sector innovation could be stimulated by an infusion of cash through market-rate loans with a deferred payback provision (to cover deficit spending during the initial period of R&D). If an entity is unable or unwilling to honor its loan obligations, then all associated R&D and productization shall become public domain. Basically, the government can invest in clean energy, etc. with the expectation that the taxpayers will, at some point, either be *paid back* for the use of their money or, in the alternative, have *unrestricted access* to the fruits of the research and development. An obvious exception to this approach would be in the case of advanced weapons development. I really don't think we need to provide the general public with the schematics for a thermonuclear device. After all, the *Internet* already *does* that!

Now, if the government has a *real* need to meddle in business, why not pressure the *existing* regulatory agencies to do their jobs? Today, FINRA and the SEC do a great job of harassing and fining small, honest financial planning companies for trivial violations (often based on conflicting interpretations of the regulations) ... because they *can!* At the same time, they can't seem to catch the Bernie Madoffs of the world until a few billion dollars have disappeared. At least the SEC has an excuse: its staff members' may have been distracted and suffering from eyestrain from watching porn on the Internet. So, here's my Platform's recommendation: either do your job or get replaced by *someone* or *something* that's more effective.

The same goes for the Financial Accounting Standards Board (FASB). I've already discussed its great decision-making when it came to Enron's use of the *"mark-to-market"* principle, but here's another hint: business performance cannot be legitimately compared within the context of *Generally Accepted Accounting Principles* (GAAP). There's just too wide a variance with respect to GAAP treatments. Depending upon how two *identically* performing companies choose to reflect their financials within GAAP, you could get two *wildly different* sets of results ... all *"within Generally Accepted Accounting Principles."* Essentially, annual reports, 10Ks, 10Qs, etc. are somewhat meaningless. As a result, a lot of the FINRA and SEC requirements that pertain to creating an *"informed investor"* are just an intellectual trip to *Fantasy Island*. So, let's throw something into the Platform for radically reducing the variance between GAAP treatments, so that a more accurate baseline can be established. This would not only help individual investors with their analyses, but it would go a long way toward reducing the *massive* failure rate among mergers and acquisitions ... *all* of which would help the economy.

This Platform has also previously addressed establishing an indexed-budget for the Federal government (indexed to economic cycles and population shifts) that will be funded through a Flat Tax. Again, that combination will free up cash for businesses and individuals to reinvest. Rather than constraining business expansion and discretionary spending, this approach will stimulate both. There is *no* reason that businesses and individuals should be required to abdicate such decisions to the Federal government, which is exactly what excessive taxation and regulation does. Raise your hand if you think someone *else* has the right to make decisions for *you*. If you have your hand up ... good news ... you're *really* going to like Health Care Reform!

While I'm on a roll, let's solve what the Trouble Assets Relief Program (TARP) marginally tried to address and what a small piece of the Wall Street Reform Bill is going to try to regulate. Let me go on record as saying that I'm *not* for bailouts. There should be consequences for the decisions we make. While I appreciate the fact that some people suffered substantial losses in funds that were *"too good to be true,"* had the blended securities somehow performed, I rather doubt that *"reform"* would be on the table. The same goes for the foreclosures that have resulted from individuals accepting home loans for which they were *clearly* unqualified. Should there be reform? *Yes!* Does it require new agencies, hundreds of thousands of pages of new regulations, and countless years of ensuing litigation? *No!* It just requires *common sense*. Figure out what went wrong; fix it; try to recover assets from those who were unjustly enriched; and proportionately distribute the recovery among the victims. If the victims don't fully recover their losses ... well, people are generally willing to pay for an education, so chalk it up as an educational expense.

- Do I feel sorry for most of the people who just tried to take advantage of deals that shouldn't have passed their *"smell test?" No!* Next time, pay attention to the *"smell."*
- Do I feel bad for the business impact on banks that were forced by community organizers and government threats (*i.e.,* the withholding of funds) to ignore sound business

practices? *No!* Next time, develop a backbone and do what you *know* is right.
- Do I feel bad for the elected officials who pushed through the Fannie Mae and Freddie Mac legislation that built the foundation for the collapse? Do you even *need* to ask? And please note that these same individuals shifted the blame and then had the nerve to use the debacle for political gain ... while *again* cutting a special deal for Fannie Mae and Freddie Mac. In my opinion, people like this *do* deserve *lifetime* appointments to government jobs ... perhaps something to do with the manufacturing of license plates might be in order.

As for controlling CEO compensation and executive bonuses, I don't think that's any of the Federal government's business. What is *really* needed is a more *interested* and *informed* investor population and an *independent* Compensation Committee ... rather than one made up of the CEO's *Board cronies*. If you need a benchmark, why not use the Presidency. I don't care how complex a private sector business is, I doubt that it's as challenging as being *"Leader of the Free World."* At some point, investors are going to realize this. The days of $50+ million compensations packages for CEOs will dissipate as soon as investors realize that the majority of that money could either have been distributed in the form of dividends or used to expand the business. Can you say, *"job creation?"* Of course, the Compensation Committees will have to stop playing the same losing game that's been perfected by professional sports franchise owners, who inexplicably keep raising the *ante* in fear of losing a *star* player. This is akin to bidding against yourself in an auction. Someday soon, the *"light bulb"* is going to go on ... and the owners (and stockholders) are going to realize that that player or CEO really doesn't have a lot of other *"career options"* that would pay the type of compensation that's being *squandered* today. When that happens, the winners will be the economy, the consumer, and the investors who funded the opportunity in the first place.

I could go on, but I think it should already be obvious that there are *a lot* of options we could explore within both the public *and* the private sectors that would help move our economy forward in a positive direction. I think Walt Kelly, creator of the Pogo comic strip, had it right when he satirically rephrased Commander Perry's famous quote into the classic line: *"We have met the enemy and he is us."*

CITIZENSHIP

Now that we've stimulated some thought on the Economy, let's tackle the issue of Citizenship. Notice that I said *"Citizenship"* rather than *"Immigration"* because our Nation's issues aren't limited to Immigration Reform. Clearly identifying who is a citizen and what their responsibilities are as citizens is relevant to every *legitimate* legislative issue that qualifies as *"general Welfare"* and passes the *"necessary and proper"* test. That determination will dramatically effect who's covered, how much it will cost, and who's on the hook to pay for the government programs that are justified under Article I, Section 8. But since Immigration Reform seems to be on everyone's mind, let's start with that.

Immigration Reform: "Documented" Illegality

Sensitivity to the use of the term *"illegal alien"* within the context of citizenship is *"political correctness"* at its worst. There is a *legal* way to enter this country. In the *absence* of entering it *legally*, you have ... by default ... entered it *illegally*. End of story!

Trying to make ourselves *"feel better"* by calling those who enter our country *illegally* by a *kinder, gentler* term ... such *"undocumented worker"* ... is nothing more than mental masturbation. It doesn't change the reality, and it is a clear misrepresentation of fact.

Here's a news flash: not every *"undocumented"* person who enters our country does so to *work* ... at least within *my* definition, which is limited to include *legal* (oh, gosh ... there's that word again) employment. Now, if you want to include *illegal* work in your definition ... well, I guess *everyone* who subverts the system to come to this country *is* an *"undocumented worker."* I *suppose* drug dealers and their runners *do* come to *work* in our country. *Terrorist operatives* in sleeper cells probably do as well. So, if we don't restrict our discussion to *legitimate* work, I guess all of you who think I'm insensitive for using the term *"illegal aliens"* are right! However, the fact remains: all of your *"undocumented workers"* are still *"illegal."*

Still not convinced? Let's compare the *Human Pipeline* that flows between the Mexican and U.S. border to the Oil Pipelines that environmentalists are so adamantly against. Of course, Oil Pipelines stimulate economic growth; but then, so does the Human Pipeline. In fact, it is estimated that between *$18-39 billion* a year in drug money is generated and laundered through the Human Pipeline. Top that BP! And there are no accidental spills with which to contend. Well, then again ... actually, there *are*. As illegal aliens enter our great Nation and trek through the National Parks on our border, they leave an estimated 8-16 *tons* of trash behind on an annual basis (almost none of which is biodegradable). This includes thousands of plastic food and water containers as well as articles of clothing ... including an occasional jacket with some sort of foreign designer label on it; one that says *al-Qaeda*. And I fear the day that one of them accidentally starts a forest fire. It's only a matter of time. I'm hoping the Sierra Club, *et al.* will jump on board with me to stop the flow of illegal immigrants ... *at least* on a basis of protecting our environment.

Since apologizing has become *"in vogue"* recently, I'll begin by apologizing to those who have *earned* the right to become *naturalized* citizens of the United States. *You* do not deserve to have your status *denigrated* by the siren call of *"political correctness."* You represent everything that is good about being a citizen of our country. You waited your turn, followed the rules, and were rewarded with the greatest gift that our Constitution can bestow upon you. The vast majority of you choose to wholly embrace the culture of the United States, which includes a *degree* of retention of your *native* culture to enrich our diversity. However, you are proud to be Americans and take your citizenship seriously. Sometimes, those of us who were blessed with our citizenship by virtue of our birth, fail to appreciate the value of the gift we have received as completely as you do. So, I will apologize for that as well.

CSC's Platform Position: **This Platform holds to the doctrine that ... if you are immigrating to the United States ... do it *legally*. Otherwise, you are asserting a right that you do *not* have under the law.**

If you are the Federal government and want to assert your *preemptive* right relative to establish and administer immigration law through the Supremacy Clause of the Constitution

(Article VI, Section 2), then assume the associated responsibility to *enforce* it. And do *not* waste precious time and resources, including taxpayers' dollars, to litigate against States that try to *assist* you in this regard. Instead, if you must litigate, take action against *lesser* officials who create *"Sanctuary Cities"* that fly in the face of your authority; cities that *proactively disregard* Federal law on a *selective* basis in the name of *"political correctness."* If *"political correctness"* has standing within the context of the *Constitution*, then *show* me ... because no matter how many times I have read that document, I have never been able to find it.

If we're going to revoke the *"Don't Ask, Don't Tell"* rule (a.k.a., Defense Directive 1304.26, which was passed under the Clinton Administration in 1993), let's not *reapply* it to immigration (... or to the interrogation of terrorist suspects either). If a law enforcement officer stops someone based upon probable cause associated with the commission of a crime, that officer shall have the *authority* and *responsibility* to ask the suspect to produce *any* documentation required by State or Federal law (just as our citizens are required to do when they travel abroad). Such suspects, who are here *legally*, just have to produce the required documentation. If such suspects are *not* here *legally*, they'll be rewarded with an all-expenses-paid trip back to their country of origin unless we decide to prosecute them for the crime for which they were initially detained (*i.e.,* Jaywalking, parking violation, etc.? *No!* ... Rape, murder, drug trafficking, etc.? *Yes!*).

For those who make the argument that it is *inherently racist* to ask for documentation, I offer two recommendations. First, look in the mirror. *You* basically *believe* that an *inherent* difference exists between law enforcement officers and the general population and that this difference somehow *perverts* law enforcement officers' ability to conduct themselves within prescribed guidelines. In effect, you are implying that *your* ethics, as a member of the general population, are superior to *theirs*. Now, go look up the definition of *"racism."* You are applying your *own* personal *bias* to an entire class of people and attributing a negative behavior to them. Of course, *you're* not a racist because law enforcement officers come in all shapes, sizes and *colors*. *You're* just *ignorantly biased!*

Secondly, don't travel abroad. All of those Eurasian countries that you think are so *"culturally sophisticated"* as compared to the United States are *far* more demanding when it comes to travel documentation. And forget about taking that *romantic trip* to Central or South America unless you're willing to be questioned on a random basis. I also hear that they're not that *big* on needing *"probable cause"* to stop you ... or to *arrest* you for that matter.

That being said, I will be the first to admit that our present immigration process is a *glowing* representation of how *convoluted* and *dysfunctional* our agency processes can be. So, in an effort to improve the process, this Platform calls for the following:

- *Student and Travel Visas* shall remain unchanged *except* ... if you allow your Student or Travel Visas to lapse, you will be found and deported; no more *dissolving* into the general population without accountability. More than a few terrorists have used this method to become *"lost"* among our general population, and *this* Platform will *not* allow that scenario to continue. There's a *"right"* and a *"wrong"* way to enter and remain in this country. If you enter it the *right* way: no problem. If you enter it the *wrong* way, we're going to presume you have a reason for avoiding the law, and we're going to hunt you down and deport you.
- *Work Visas* shall be granted for *specific* jobs with *specific* employers upon review and approval of related petitions.
  - Each such visa shall be granted for an appropriate period, not to exceed one year.
  - At all times, the visa recipient shall remain in good standing with both his or her employer as well as within the context of adhering to the laws of the United States.
  - Extensions may be sought no *less* than 60 days before the natural expiration of the visa.

- o Immigration and Naturalization Services (INS) shall have no *more* than 30 days to consider such petitions for extension and decide whether they should be granted.
- o At the conclusion of five continuous years of residence within the United States under appropriate work visas, an individual may petition to become a naturalized citizen.
- INS (in cooperation with law enforcement agencies) shall conduct a *thorough* background check and administer a citizenship test, *in English*, to the applicant.
- Upon successful completion of the background check and receipt of a passing grade with respect to the citizenship test, such individual shall be sworn in as a naturalized citizen of the United States.

With respect to the 13 million *"illegal aliens"* who currently reside within the United States, I call for the following:

- Those who would like to pursue the path to citizenship shall be permitted to apply for one of the visas described above, and the United States shall, on a *one-time* basis, waive any associated country quota limitation upon application for citizenship. For those who might claim that this is *unfair* or *racist* in any way ... it isn't! It shouldn't represent an inconvenience of *any* kind to those whom you have defined as *"undocumented workers"* because, by definition, they already must have jobs through which they can apply for Work Visas.
  - o And in the spirit of correcting this problem once and for all, I'd even waive prosecution of those businesses that knowingly hired *"illegal aliens"* if they assumed *responsibility* for those who petitioned for Work Visas.
  - o Thereafter, businesses that knowingly hire *"illegal aliens"* will be considered to have aided and abetted the commission of a felony, and the associated fines and imprisonment shall be punitive in nature.
- There shall be also be a path for *"illegal alien minors"* of good moral character (similar to the DREAM Act established under the Bush Administration) to pursue citizenship if their parent/parents or guardian either have

secured or are pursuing citizenship or if such *"illegal alien minor"* shall choose to independently pursue citizenship provided that they have graduated in good standing from an American high school and either: (a) petition for a Work Visa; (b) petition for a Student Visa; or (c) enlist in the United States military and serve honorably for a period of not less than *two* years, at which time they may petition for citizenship (just as they could in either of the other two categories at the culmination of *five* years).
- This Platform also calls for a discontinuation of the status of *"Permanent Resident"* in favor of the streamlined process described above and the more definitive commitment required by a petitioning for citizenship. If the United States is going to be your residence of choice for the rest of your life, then become a citizen.
- This Platform also calls for revisiting the efficacy of Section 1 of the Fourteenth Amendment, which was passed in 1868 and provides (in part): *"All persons born or naturalized in the United States, and subject to the jurisdiction thereof, are citizens of the United States and of the State wherein they reside."* This provision has apparently created a cottage industry on this country's southwest border where pregnant women wait on the border until delivery is imminent, then rush over the border to deliver their children on U.S. soil so that the child can claim United States citizenship (a.k.a., *"anchor babies"*). This was never the intent of the Amendment, and it now has produced an added complication to enforcing immigration laws. Deciding whether to deport illegal alien parents whose children are, by application of the Fourteenth Amendment, citizens of the United States is a contentious issue. This natural and compassionate hesitancy to enforce our immigration laws in such cases has unfortunately created a gaping hole in our immigration strategy that many foreigners intentionally exploit.
  - If this were the rule of law everywhere, what would happen if a baby was born prematurely on a flight over the Pacific? Would the child be a citizen of the Pacific Ocean? Would the child be a citizen of the next closest

island/country? Or would the child be a citizen of the country from which its parents were citizens (*i.e.*, the culture within which the child would most likely be raised)? Why not just apply *common sense?*
- **And did I mention that under this Platform, you can't *vote* unless you're *actually* a citizen in good standing ... and alive? It's a throwback to the *Constitution* that this Platform is going to keep in place.**
 So *there* ... problem solved!

Before I close out this Section, I would like to give a special shout out to Arizona. Thanks for trying to *"provide for the common Defense"* of your residents, even though it wasn't apparently the *"politically correct"* thing to do.

It's interesting to note that, in 2007, Missouri residents overwhelmingly passed an Amendment to their State Constitution that declared English to be the official language of the State. All governmental proceedings in Missouri are now *required* to be conducted *exclusively* in English, and *no one* can demand government services in *any other language*. Imagine ... in today's world ... the audacity of those people!

But wait ... there's more!

In 2008, the *"Show Me"* State showed Arizona how it's done. They passed a bill that requires their law enforcement officers to verify the immigration status of *any* person that's arrested and to notify Federal authorities if an individual is found to be in this country illegally. The shock and horror of it all! Look out, Phillipsburg and Conception Junction ... San Francisco and Los Angeles are *probably* going to stop doing business with your towns now that they know.

Oh, and did I mention that Missouri passed *another* law in 2009 that precludes Missouri's Department of Higher Education from knowingly awarding financial assistance to students who are in this country illegally?

So, where is the media when we need it? Where is the ACLU? Where are all the civil rights activists? Why hasn't the White House condemned the State of Missouri and instructed the Department of Justice to file a suit against the good people of Missouri? I guess it's possible that no one's read the laws in detail yet, but *that* didn't stop them when it came to Arizona. No, by golly ... heads should have been rolling by now!

Hmmm ... you don't suppose that no one raised a ruckus because Missouri's not a *border* State, do you? And what does that have to do with it, you ask? Well, interior States like Missouri don't have a lot of *illegal aliens* in their midst to flood the streets in protest. *No* protests ... *no* media coverage; *no* media coverage ... *no "photo ops"* or *"sound bites ops"* to use to draw attention to yourself, your Party, or your *"special interest"* group. *Now*, do you *understand* why everyone in Missouri is just smiling at the rest of us?

So, my advice to Arizona is to *relocate* your State *inland*. Your proximity to the border is putting your residents at risk, exploding your crime rate, generating negative publicity and false accusations of racism, and driving other *"politically correct"* States, businesses and people to discontinue their contact with you. Okay, that *last* point is probably a *positive* ... but the other ones *aren't* good! Relocating your State is your only hope.

But wait a minute ... what if we were to add Mexico as a State to push the problem further south? The border with Belize and Guatemala is smaller and would be easier to control. But why stop there? If we roll in a few more countries, divided Panama into North and South Panama (kind of like the Koreas), and only add *North* Panama as a State, we'd only have to monitor the *Panama Canal* to control our southern border. Quick, get the President on the phone! I think I have an idea that even *his* political team will like. Besides, there are a lot of *"oppressed minorities"* in those countries we'd have to incorporate as States, and that spells *votes* for the Democratic Party!

FOREIGN POLICY

<u>No Apologies Needed</u>

Although it's apparently the *"in"* thing to do, I am *not* going to apologize for the United States' past foreign policy decisions. However, I *will* admit that our foreign policy *has* had a potentially *negative* impact on effective *global* communication. Were it not for the United States, the entire world might be speaking German.

That being said, I am hard pressed to find an example of a country that has had a more positive impact on the world. If a few foreign leaders feel obligated to criticize the United States on occasion, consider the source ... and then refer back to my initial discussion of the *Seven Deadly Sins*. This displeasure with the United States can often be tied to some combination of

Pride, Avarice/Greed, Envy, Wrath/Anger, Lust, Gluttony, and Sloth on behalf of the disgruntled foreign leader.

The United States is providing about $26 billion a year to foreign countries. The preponderance of the money that we give to the top four recipients (Israel, Egypt, Pakistan and Jordan) is for weapons and military equipment upgrades. Israel spends about 75% of its funds to buy U.S. weapons, so at least we get some return on our investment there. We're not as fortunate with regard to where the other countries spend their money, but hey, it's for a good cause ... helping arm potentially militant countries.

Speaking of good causes, I have less of a problem with the remainder of our foreign aid as it tends to provide health and educational assistance to countries like Kenya, South Africa, Mexico, Columbia, Nigeria and the Sudan (in that order). Still, I am concerned that *all* of the countries to which we provide aid ... with the *exception* of Israel ... have consistently voted *against* our position on critical issues within the United Nations (on average: they vote against us about 75% of the time). We're not getting much *"bang for the buck"* if you know what I mean.

There's also a segment of the United States that *resembles* a Third World Country. About 15% of our population is illiterate and about 12.5% lives in poverty. You have to wonder what would happen if we temporarily suspended our foreign aid and redirected the $26 billion to address illiteracy and poverty *in the United States.*

Oh, I know what some of you are thinking: *"The Common Sense Czar is some sort of xenophobic, ultranationalist."* I'm really not. I just think that it makes *common sense* to explore alternatives. We know that the foreign aid we are distributing (other than to Israel) is *not* generating a desirable level of support on the international issues that we consider to be important. Therefore, let's spend the $26 billion within the United States to see if we can eliminate (or at least, dramatically reduce) illiteracy and poverty within *our* country and do some other good things. It's a more *controllable* environment, it has a more immediate impact on our society, and ... if we prove that we knew how to do it in our own backyard, maybe foreign leaders would begin to *admire* us and seek our counsel rather than admonish us and expect our apologies.

Don't look at this as *Isolationism*; look at it as a *different form* of foreign aid. All you have to do is pretend that those individuals who are living within the United States under Third World conditions are really *foreigners*. It shouldn't be much of a stretch of your imagination if you've ever viewed the conditions of which I speak.

 **CSC's Platform Position:** This Platform calls for a temporary moratorium on foreign aid other than any such aid for which we are already contractually committed to provide (*i.e.*, I believe we should honor our word). The only possible exception would be for countries that continually demonstrate their support of our ideals (*e.g.*, Australia, Canada, England, Israel and a few others). If a country has our back, we should have theirs.

This Platform believes that we should take a hard look at the amount of aid we provide to *other* countries. One can only assume that our assistance hasn't been particularly effective ... or even well received ... since our current Administration feels compelled to apologize for our country and its arrogance. Now, I could be cynical and think that those apologies were merely made for *political* purposes, but let's suppose for a minute that they weren't. That means we can look at making *substantive* cuts in the assistance we provide to the rest of the world. Of course, the political downside is ... if we think they hate us *now*, just wait until the *freebies* go away!

Taking politics out of it for the moment ... helping others just *feels* like the right thing to do. It's consistent with the Christian beliefs upon which this Nation was built (*"One Nation under God ... In God We Trust ... etc."*). But wait! That gives us even *another* reason to reevaluate our foreign aid expenditures. We've been informed that we are no longer to refer to ourselves as a Christian nation. So be it. Wow, that's going to make it even easier to drift toward the isolationist period we are probably going to have to experience to dig our way out of the trillions of dollars of debt that we've miraculously created between over the last few years.

Then, we will redeploy the aid we *would* have spent in foreign countries within our *own* country. This Platform calls for providing training to those United States citizens who are illiterate or living in poverty. Of Course, we will *not* be able to help *all* of them raise their standards of living because they have the freedom of choice to *remain* illiterate or to live in poverty. However, it would be wonderful to look *within* our country rather than *outside* of our country *first*.

And just so you don't think that I'm naïve, I do recognize that the national *"photo ops"* might not be as *compelling* as standing beside impoverished children in some far away land ... and that *some* people might find it to be *less* rewarding to solve *our* Nation's problems than to provide their unappreciated meddling in another country's issues. After all, that's why our *celebrities* can't adopt *American* orphans and our politicians prefer junkets to *remote* corners of the Earth as opposed to visits to areas within the United States that might otherwise make them *uncomfortable*. But remember: this Platform has already done away with *"political correctness,"* so it's focus is on *results* rather than *rhetoric*; on making *others* feel good rather than just ourselves; on spending *taxpayer money* as provided for in the *Constitution* rather than in ways that panders to reelection and self-aggrandizement. And if this conversation makes you a bit uncomfortable ... good! As Eldridge Cleaver once said when he was a leading member of the Black Panther Party *"If you're not part of the solution ... you're part of the problem."* Just as an aside, Mr. Cleaver later became a born-again Christian and joined the Republican Party ... perhaps as a testimony to the sincerity of his quote.

Then, let's also take some of this *"found money,"* and redirect it to better compensate those who place their lives *"in harm's way"* to protect our freedoms, our lives and our property. This Platform calls for an increase in compensation for:
- Combat Troops
- Active Law Enforcement Officers, and
- First Responders (*e.g.*, Firefighters, etc.).

These latter two groups shouldn't *need* union representation to feel that their *"best interests"* are being protected. We should acknowledge their importance and act accordingly. Otherwise, politicians will continue to use this part of the public sector as a pawn to try to control us (*i.e.*, *"We'll have to start firing police officers and firefighters unless you approve/reject the XYZ Bill, tax, bond issue, etc."*); and unions will continue to use it to establish undue influence among the politicians (*i.e.*, *"We won't support your legislation or election campaign unless you do the following for us ..."*). It's an unseemly element of our political environment that needs to be *shut down*.

And while we're at it, this Platform supports providing unique educational benefits to individuals who serve in these positions as well; a sort of extension of the GI Bill to make sure that we attract individuals to these services that are worthy of our support. As we elevate the public perception of these positions, we will concurrently reduce the fears of racism and bias that have been raised in the past. Accordingly, we will be in a position to support a zero tolerance policy for violations that offend *common sense*. And we can do *all* of this because the rest of the world apparently hates us. There really is a *silver lining* to every cloud!

Afghanistan, Iraq and Terrorism

I think we should sit down with terrorists without imposing any preconditions, and try to use diplomacy to persuade them to stop killing themselves and innocent people ... or, at least, the innocent people. Surely, diplomacy is the way to go! It will heighten respect for our country, and I might even get a Nobel Peace Prize out of it. If I were President, I would send an engraved invitation to Osama Bin Laden to come to my home for a Beer Summit ... if *only* I had his address.

Okay, you can stop laughing now. I had just been singing along with *Hey Jude* on the radio, and I had a *"Presidential moment."* The singing took away my breath, and I apparently lacked sufficient oxygen to think clearly. Now, for what I really believe. Remember our discussion about the Eighth Amendment as it pertained to *"cruel and unusual punishment?"* Well, brace yourself!

CSC's Platform Position: This Platform calls for a phased withdrawal from Afghanistan and Iraq ... on an *undisclosed* timetable. I think we have helped those countries to the degree that we can. And within the context of *"you can lead a horse to water, but you can't make him drink"* ... it's time to see if the horse is thirsty. This position will improve our relationships with a few foreign countries (for those who care); it will bring our troops home and take them out of harm's way; and it will allow us to redirect our time and energy to solving our country's problems. The billions of dollars that can be redirected toward *appropriate* Federal programs and to *retire* national debt will come at time when we have a great need to conserve cash.

Of course, there are those who will say that withdrawal from these foreign lands will bring the *War Against Terror* to our own shores. This Platform is quite sensitive to that. As a result, it also calls for a policy to be put in place and communicated *clearly* to the rest of the world: *"Don't Tread On US!"* More specifically:

TO WHOM IT MAY CONCERN: *Any* act of aggression against the United States or its citizens will be dealt with *swiftly* and *severely*. We will *not* ask for any other country's *permission* ... or *wait* for a *consensus* of support. We *will* respond *disproportionately* to any act of terrorism and use *every* resource available to us to *completely eliminate* the root cause ... as we would with any other plague that might threaten the *"Life, Liberty and pursuit of Happiness"* of which our citizens are guaranteed.

I call this my *"Tom Jones"* interpretation of the *Eighth Amendment:* ♫ *"It's not un-u-su-al to be-head a ter-ror-ist ... They do it to our own after they beat them with their fists ..."* ♫

I don't mean to be macabre, but I've just grown a little insensitive to individuals who perpetrate acts of violence against innocent victims. So, under this Platform's interpretation of the Bill of Rights, *terrorists* will *not* be given the rights of our citizens ... *period!* Try to blow up a plane ... don't expect to receive a Miranda Warning. Your *"right to remain silent"* officially stopped when you decided to detonate an explosive device in an attempt to kill hundreds of innocent people. I'll provide the water *and* the board ... and we'll find out more about those additional attacks you promised were coming before you have the opportunity to *"lawyer up."*

Speaking of confessions: if you confess to planning the attack on 9/11 (as Khalid Sheikh Mohammed did) ... don't expect me to authorize spending $100 million to try you in a civilian court in New York so the world will think we're a kinder, gentler Nation. You're a *terrorist* ... *not* a civilian. In fact, I wouldn't even waste time and money trying you before a Military Tribunal. During these tough economic times, I'd just authorize $100 for a few rounds of .50 caliber ammunition and make a Navy Seal count to 10 while you try to escape in an open field.

And speaking of Navy Seals, this Platform is not going to court martial military personnel serving in a combat zone for *allegedly* punching a terrorist during (or after) his or her capture (as was done based upon a complaint *filed* by Ahmed Hashim Abed). As I recall, Ahmed Hashim Abed was the mastermind behind the ambush of four Blackwater agents who were transporting supplies for a catering company. *His* victims were killed by gunfire and grenades. Then, their bodies were *burned* and *dragged* through the city. Two of the victims' bodies were then hung on a bridge over the Euphrates River to create a *"photo op"* for the world press. No, I'm not going to authorize expensive court martial proceedings for the Navy Seals. Instead, I'm going to authorize a few dollars for some really nice medals to pin on their chests and give them each a pair of Everlast boxing gloves, personally autographed by Rocky.

- Just as a level set: the number of U.S. combat troops who have been captured in Iraq and Afghanistan and returned by the enemy alive ... is approximately zero. What goes around comes around. We just need to be consistent so the *"punishment"* isn't considered to be *"unusual."*

Now, just so you don't get the idea that I'm some kind of violent or vindictive Czar ... I'm not. I just care more about protecting the lives of *innocent* individuals than I do about creating *new* rights for those who would *intentionally* and *viciously* attack them. This Platform's recommendation for punishing terrorists is to parallel *their* treatment of prisoners when it comes time to sentence them. After all, there isn't a more direct way of determining what they think is *"kosher"* in this regard (no pun intended). If they think that their actions might be applied directly to *them*, it may give them a new perspective when it comes to cutting off the heads of their live prisoners, etc.

As a friend of mine once said, *"You can't attribute rational thought to irrational behavior."* Rational people do not ascribe to killing *innocent* people … be they in Iraq, Afghanistan, or the United States. *Terrorists do not differentiate* between men, women, and children. They *do not differentiate* between military personnel and civilians. They *do not even differentiate* between those who support them … and those who don't. They just call the supporters they send to slaughter *"martyrs"* rather than what they really are … which is *"dead."*

One final point: this Platform's *common sense* definition of a *"terrorist"* is one who, either individually or in concert with others, uses or threatens to use force or violence against innocent people to intimidate or coerce ideological change. As our President would say, *"Let me be clear"* … I don't distinguish between a card-carrying member of al-Qaeda, a lunatic psychiatrist in the military, and a terribly misguided citizen who would blow up a building in Oklahoma City. In my book, they're *all* terrorists … and now, you know how the *National Platform of Common Sense* would deal with them.

The United Nations

One of our Nation's *worst* Progressive leaders … oh, I'm sorry … I meant *first* Progressive leaders (just a Freudian slip) was Woodrow Wilson. He was the champion of the League of Nations, which served as a precursor to today's United Nations. The League of Nations was spawned by the Part I of the *Treaty of Versailles*. It was envisioned as an inter-governmental forum tasked with preventing war and settling international disputes through diplomatic negotiations. It was to foster a world that would embrace disarmament and promote human rights while curtailing drug and arms trafficking … among other laudable goals. It had 58 members at the height of its glory, which included Adolf Hitler and Benito Mussolini until they decided that they didn't like the idea.

It's worth noting that President Wilson was *so* successful in advocating the necessity of the League of Nations that the United States never bothered to join. Alas, he was still rewarded for his efforts when he *won* the Nobel Peace Prize ... apparently for his *promise*.

Enter the United Nations Organization, which was formed in 1945 after those truculent dictators, Adolf Hitler and Benito Mussolini, had been summarily dispatched. Similar to the League of Nations, the U.N. was created to form an international community that would work together in a cooperative manner to maintain peace as well as championing economic, environmental and human rights initiatives throughout the world. This organization is made up of 192 countries; five of which (China, France, Russia, United Kingdom, and United States) are permanent members of the Security Council with the ability to veto any non-procedural resolution.

The United Nations essentially is funded by what amounts to a *"progressive tax."* While the United States represents 0.5% of the United Nations' membership, it is privileged to provide the beautiful New York City facility in which the U.N. is hosted and fund approximately 22% of the U.N.'s general budget and 27% of its budget for peacekeeping forces. Such a deal!

In return, we get reprimanded for *our* human rights violations for using drone aircraft to kill terrorists. We're right up there with China, Iran and North Korea. Well, maybe a little *below* Iran since *it* was elected to the U.N.'s *Commission on the Status of Women*; a four-year appointment to the influential human rights body. That's the *same* Iran that operates as a theocratic state in which stoning women to death for committing adultery is enshrined in law and lashings are required for women judged to be *"immodest."* Good call, U.N.!

The U.N.'s Human Rights Council, which criticized us, is dominated by a bloc of Islamic and African states, who are supported by China, Cuba and Russia ... absolute role models of Human Rights. It even features Sudan among its members; you know, the *same* Sudan that has practiced *"ethnic cleansing"* in Darfur by launching horrific, ongoing acts of genocide against its Black population. I guess the old phrase is correct: *"It takes one to know one."*

In any event, with every passing year, it becomes *more* of a privilege to pay a *disproportionate* amount of the U.N.'s operating costs for such *fair* and *balanced* support. And as I mentioned earlier, with the exception of Israel, the other countries to which we distribute significant foreign aid *routinely* vote *against* our position on *substantive* resolutions within the U.N. Those of you who support the concept and consequences of *"progressive taxation"* are undoubtedly *perfectly fine* with this scenario. Those of you who have a sense of *equity* probably aren't as keen about it.

 **CSC's Platform Position:** It's time to *use* the indoor plumbing ... or remove ourselves from the porcelain throne. This Platform supports its *own* U.N. Resolution:

"Dear United Nations: either convincingly demonstrate the ability to remove extreme political biases from your procedural and substantive resolutions ... and to apply common sense ... or figure out where you're going to relocate and how you're going to pay for all of your global summits in exotic locations ... because this is the end of La Dolce Vita."

GLOBAL ENVIRONMENTAL ISSUES

The environment can be viewed from a global *and* domestic basis. I hate to burst anyone's bubble, but the global issue is really *outside* of our control. Oh sure, we can make recommendations, and the rest of the world might follow a few of them as long as they are disproportionately funded by the United States (... kind of like the U.N.), but by-and-large, the rest of the world is going to do what *it* wants to do. Evolving Nations are going to be more concerned about *jobs* than they are *Global Warming*. And while *we* may pay good money to watch a much-hyped documentary that features a boring individual's interpretation of an enormously complex and unsettled area of science ... and an area in which the presenter has absolutely *no* level of *expertise* ... the rest of the world probably isn't *quite* as excited. *Actual* experts have widely disparate opinions with regard to the validity of the threat of *Global Warming*. And it seems the Oscar-winning presenter may have *"massaged"* some of the facts in an attempt to have a *"happy ending."*

Then, *Mother Nature* flexed her muscles with the volcanic eruption of *Eyjafjallajökull* (sorry, I couldn't resist *daring* you to pronounce it), and we came to learn that this single event released 150,000 – 300,000 *tons* of CO_2 into the atmosphere *each day* (one of those dreaded *"greenhouse"* gases we've been warned about). We obviously need a Global Conference on Volcanic Eruptions ... perhaps somewhere exotic ... where thousand of people can fly and then rent cars to drive to the Conference as well as all the embassy-like after-parties. It's clear we need *immediate* legislation that *bans* volcanic eruptions!

If you think I'm kidding, Nancy Pelosi led an impressive delegation from the United States to the U.N. Climate Change Conference in Copenhagen at the beginning of 2010. The Speaker approved twenty other Congressmen (15 Democrats and 6 Republicans total) and 38 staff members to attend with her. I'm not sure why Congressmen need two staffers each to accompany them on a trip of this nature, but former Senator and Presidential candidate John Edwards assures me that it is standard procedure. Apparently, it has something to do with having one to hold the camera.

When you add the Senators that chose to attend and *their* staff members, you pass the 100 mark. That doesn't include spouses and family members who took advantage of the *"free"* trip as well. Initial estimates indicate that the *"free"* trip only cost taxpayers $1.1 million ... not including the cost of President Obama and his entourage, who also visited the event.

Perhaps, the 100+ people in the delegation are the individuals the President was admonishing in his State of the Union speech when he said, *"I know that there are those who disagree with the overwhelming scientific evidence on climate change."* I mean, why else would all these people travel to Copenhagen for a Climate Change Conference other than to be educated on the issue. They certainly didn't *contribute* in any meaningful way. The Conference itself has been described as a *"disappointing failure."*

Clearly, most of these people must disagree with the premise that climate change is an issue. After all, it took three U.S. military jets, two 737s and Speaker Pelosi's Gulfstream V to transport the bulk of the delegation to the Conference, while 59 other members flew on commercial airlines. The President's attendance means that Air Force One, a spare identical plane, and several cargo planes also made the trip. That means our delegation created a carbon footprint that would make Sasquatch feel inadequate.

Didn't these people know that *Al Gore* had already spoken at the event during its first few days? Do we really need anything beyond the prognostications of the *"Father of the Internet?"* My goodness, he's even got an Oscar! If that isn't *"overwhelming scientific evidence,"* I don't know what is. Big Al told the world that, *"These figures are fresh. Some of the models suggest to Dr. Maslowski that there is a 75 per cent chance that the entire north polar ice cap, during the summer months, could be completely ice-free within five to seven years."* Unfortunately, this apparently came as a *total* surprise to Dr. Maslowski who refuted the comments almost immediately in a separate interview. On the bright side, maybe there's another movie in this ... perhaps a comedy!

 **CSC's Platform Position:** This Platform calls for the elimination U.S. politicians' participation in

Global Conferences on *Global Warming* since they have *little-to-no* personal *expertise*. These boondoggles are just an excuse to travel to exotic locations on the taxpayers' dime. They unnecessarily add to the carbon-footprint of which *real* environmentalists are concerned, and their *only* outcome seems to be scheduling the *next* useless conference. Mind you ... these U.N.-backed events bite us twice: once for the *pointless* participation of our politicians and their rock-star entourages; and once for our 22% share of the U.N.'s operating expenses.

Secondly, this Platform calls for environmental conferences to leverage current technology. After all, Al Gore *obviously* invented the Internet to reduce the need for burning jet fuel and gasoline to exchange ideas. The least we can do is to *honor* his contribution to mankind. Therefore, in the future, all environmental conferences must be conducted through telepresence and video conferencing (*i.e.*, through the use of webcasts, Halo™ rooms, etc.). Let's see how many *real* environmentalists we have when we shut down the travel to places like Copenhagen, Honolulu, Kyoto, Naples, Singapore, and Sydney (which are already scheduled).

One thing I'm still trying to understand is the appeal to reduce CO_2 because it's a *greenhouse* gas. My confusion stems from the fact that we expel CO_2 when we breathe. Will some environmentalist try to eliminate *us* as a source of the problem? I also seem to recall that plants convert CO_2 into oxygen through photosynthesis, which creates our breathable atmosphere. The last time I checked, oxygen was considered to be a good thing to have around. I sure hope we don't reduce *too* much of the CO_2 ... or the *"greenhouse effect"* may not be our biggest issue.

DOMESTIC ENVIRONMENTAL ISSUES

Wildlife: or One Flew Over the Cuckoo's Nest

We might actually be able to make a dent in environmental issues on the home front if we can get our politicians to stop wasting serious time and money traveling abroad. And if we actually cleaned up our own act, maybe we'd have more credibility on a global basis and could serve as a *role model* rather than a *rhetoric master*.

It's too bad that our politicians in the 1800's didn't spend *more* time *learning* from the Native Americans and *less* time worrying about how to appropriate their land. Our Native American's seem to have had a much greater appreciation for our environment and a much better relationship with it. Luckily, it's not too late to take heed.

Again, *common sense* must come into play. California is certainly one of the most progressive States when it comes to environmental law. Unfortunately, its requirement of *"Environmental Impact Statements"* (in addition to the Federal requirement under the *National Environmental Policy Act*) has become a uniquely inefficient element of development that is routinely used to delay projects, add exorbitant costs to them, and generate fees for the government (to apparently squander on *other* useless things). For example: a particular construction project was shut down for months because the construction *noise* might disturb a bird that was found to be nesting in the area. Now, I'm totally sympathetic to this type of environmental decision … except for the fact that the bird was nesting at the end of an airport *runway*. So, either the data indicating that the bird was *"sensitive to noise"* was incorrect, or we're dealing with a *deaf* bird here! Again, *common sense* might have suggested *relocating* the *"sensitive"* bird to a more conducive and less dangerous area rather than shutting down the construction site.

There's also a major *drought* in Central and Southern California that's forced severe cutbacks in water usage as well as a significant increase in the associated rates. Well, there's not *really* a draught, if you restrict the term to *natural* causes. You see, a Federal Court Judge ruled that a tiny little fish (a smelt) might get caught in the water pumps up in Sacramento, so an order was issued to shut the pumps down. As a result, water reserves associated with a record snow and rainfall were no longer accessible for inhabitants of Central and Southern California and water rationing and rate hikes ensued. Many farmers faced bankruptcy and lost their land since they could no longer irrigate it, and fruit prices in America went up accordingly. Those citizens who live in the semi-arid desert regions like San Diego had to pay more and make life-style changes relative to water usage … to *accommodate* the smelt.

Of course, no one can claim this was a politically motivated decision because *smelt* don't vote or pay taxes. This was merely an application of environmental law at its finest. Impacted citizens just haven't been smart enough to have the decision overturned on appeal. I think it would be fairly easy to do. Just claim *racial discrimination*. You see, I'm guessing that a lot of *"un-documented workers"* lost their jobs when the orchards went out of business. This is a clear case of racial profiling since the judge could *reasonably foresee* that a lot of illegal aliens might be picking the fruit. Let's organize some pickets, call the mainstream media, and get the Department of Justice to file suit against itself. Problem solved!

CSC's Platform Position: This Platform calls for educating our children to appreciate the environment (it's probably too late for the rest of us) but to do so in a way that makes *common sense*. About 27,000 species become extinct *each* year ... most of which we know *nothing* about. It's called natural selection. That's not to say we should accelerate the process or even contribute to it; just that Mother Nature is going to do as she pleases, and in some case, it might behooves us to take *human* life into consideration as well.

This Platform's call to enforce Immigration Laws will also help improve our country's environment. Think about it. There are 13 million illegal aliens in the United States, and you've got to believe that most of them drive cars or trucks (with or without licenses). If you take all those vehicles off the road ... *ta da!* ... you've got cleaner air!

Natural Resources

We need to apply *"common sense"* to all of our natural resources. We can control, reduce, and possibly even eliminate some of the man-made pollution we create. This ties in nicely with wildlife preservation and health care costs. Is there any doubt that some of the 27,000 species that become extinct each year can be attributed to the negative impact of pollution? Pesticides, cleaning agents, etc. seep into our ecological system every day and become an element of nature's food supply. This same problem almost undoubtedly contributes to human health as well. How many illness and deaths can be attributed to the poisons we put into the air, the water, and the soil? What is the impact of hormonally-enhanced livestock that is raised for the carnivores among us ... or the genetically-altered fruit and vegetables consumed by the vegans that roam the Earth? We even inoculate ourselves and our children at every opportunity to provide protection from the *dreaded* pandemics that have *yet* to really surface. And who can possibly survive *a day* without subjecting themselves to the electromagnetic and microwave radiation associated with cell phones, computer and television screens, and microwave ovens (just as examples)? As a result, autism, cancer, Alzheimer's and a wide variety of other diseases have reached record levels within our population. We can and should be sensitive to protecting and preserving our fields, streams, food supply and wildlife.

And keep in mind, the government directly owns about 30% of the United States (over 650 million acres). From a Top Ten perspective, it owns approximately:
- 85% of Nevada
- 69% of Alaska
- 57% of Utah
- 53% of Oregon
- 50% of Idaho
- 48% of Arizona
- 45% of California
- 42% of Wyoming
- 42% of New Mexico, and
- 37% of Colorado.

Some of these just crack me up. I mean ... if I owned 85% of Nevada, I wouldn't be telling people *not* to *vacation* there. If I owned 48% of Arizona, I think I'd stop *suing* the State and start *enforcing* Federal laws so that *more* people would *visit* or *live* there. And if I owned 45% of California, I wouldn't tell *anyone*. They might expect me to bail them out of their current economic crisis. As the seventh or eighth largest economy in the world, they're almost *"too big to fail."*

In any event, a lot of our most pristine and unadulterated land belongs to the government. So, it shouldn't be *too* hard to protect and preserve it from the environmental calamities that *"big business"* is just waiting to exact ... as we're all conditioned to fear.

 **CSC's Platform Position:** This Platform recommends that we invest *at least* as much in researching more natural ways to enhance food and maintain health as we invest in developing artificial methods.

We also need to research the impact of technology on our health and the environment. The funding is readily available. All we have to do is cancel some of the ridiculous earmark projects that were approved with the recent Stimulus and Health Care Reform Bills. We could use those billions of dollars to create *real* jobs in sectors that would potentially improve the lives of all of our citizens. You know ... sort of in keeping with the phrase *"providing for the ... general Welfare of the United States."* It would be both *"necessary and proper"* since this is an area of research in which *"big business"* really *has* demonstrated a proclivity to suppress negative results (*i.e., "Trust us ... cigarettes are not addictive and don't cause cancer"*). Government funded research in these areas would benefit our citizens for generations to come.

ENERGY

Who Wants to Play a Round of Gulf?

Our domestic environment dovetails into a discussion of our energy policy quite nicely. Let's look our most recent catastrophe: the Gulf Oil Spill. While its immediate economic impact has been significant, we have no way of measuring the long-term damage created by this event both in terms of the food chain and the ecosystem.

Allow me to digress for just a moment. I would like to *apologize* to the people of the world for our Nation's *arrogance* (see, I'm beginning to get the hang of this). Rather than to *acknowledge* our need for assistance from the global community, we rejected it. We pretended that we did not *need* it ... and even that we did not *appreciate* it. We acted as if we *"Ugly Americans"* could handle the problem just fine! Now, we *did* strong-arm BP into pledging a minimum of $20 billion in reparations, but we did *little else* to address the spill on an expeditious manner.

Now, back to the oil spill. In one of the few acts of leadership that President Obama was able to fit in between rounds of golf, photo ops, and a Karaoke session with Paul McCartney, he issued a moratorium on oil and gas exploration in the Gulf Coast. While this immediately cost about 8,000 people their jobs and is believed to have cost more than $2 billion in regional economic activity (with potentially greater losses expected over the next year), I support it. Even though it came just about a week or two before he was to present BP with a Presidential award for its 40 year safety record, one can't be too careful.

Seriously, I *do* support the moratorium ... just in a slightly different form. I support a moratorium on *future* off-shore drilling because it makes *common sense*. We do *not* have to drill off-shore where conditions are such that an accident is more likely to happen and more difficult to resolve. Companies are only forced to build rigs in corrosive salt-water, under enormous atmospheric pressures because we're too adamant about *not* allowing them to build rigs on land ... where we can *see* them. As they say, *"Out of sight, out of mind."* To which I offer a corollary: *"If you force people to drill in places you can't see, you're out of your mind."* Hence, why not just let the companies drill in areas like ANWR (the Alaskan Wildlife Reserve), which is rich with oil and is supported by the Inupiat Eskimos who live there. Hey, and remember ... the government owns about 69% of Alaska. Other than to spite Sarah Palin, why would we ignore the opportunity?

 **CSC's Platform Position:** **This Platform supports a *permanent* ban on *new* off-shore drilling (other than for precautionary relief wells) in return for opening up the opportunity to explore oil and gas reserves on land. You know: where you can actually *observe* the process; where the rigs aren't subject to the high-pressure and corrosive salt associated with underwater exploration; and where you have at least a snowball's chance of fixing any problem that might arise.**

Alternative Energy

Just in case you think I'm overlooking the *alternative* of ... alternative energy ... I'm not! It's just that you'd have to *ignore* reality to think that a singular focus on alternative energy would solve our present energy requirements. We simply have *wasted* too much time in the past to make it an *immediate*, viable option. However, I *certainly* agree that we need to get started in earnest *today!*

Outside of Habitat for Humanity and observing a few foreign elections, President Carter's greatest contribution to our country was his recognition that we needed to move away from oil, gas and coal. Of course, the Department of Energy has been *totally* ineffective since he created it in 1977. But, hey ... why rush into things. At least we have a massive Federal agency in place with a huge budget. You can't expect it to generate results when it's only been around a little over *three* decades. Otherwise, we'd have solar energy dialed in, and we'd all be driving electric cars.

Speaking of electric cars, our nationalization of the American automobile industry is already producing results. The President himself touted GM's release of the Chevrolet Volt. As I understand it, it can travel a whole *40 miles* on a single charge and only costs about *$41,000* and change (not including tax, title and license). Compare that to a Nissan Leaf, which only can go *100 miles* on a single charge and costs a whopping *$32,000*. Don't bother doing the math. The Administration says the Volt is *"leading the way to showing how manufacturing jobs are coming right back here to the United States of America."* Oh ... and did I mention that the Nissan Leaf is *also* built in America? ... Just without government intervention.

CSC's Platform Position: This Platform *strongly* supports the research and development of alternative energy resources. Alternative energy, in turn, will protect and improve our environment over time and reduce our dependence on foreign oil. Correspondingly, our reduced dependence on foreign oil will help mitigate our associated concerns from a national security perspective. Additionally, it will alter the supply and demand curve and potentially create downward price pressure on oil, particularly impacting OPEC. As a result, Middle East countries will have less money flowing into their economies to support *discretionary* spending on things like ... you know ... *terrorism*.

The reality is that the development of alternative fuels must be conducted *in parallel* with a controlled expansion of oil, gas, and coal production in America. It is senseless to pretend that we can get to an alternative fuel environment *"cold turkey."* Trying to tax or otherwise fine fossil fuels out of existence is senseless.

This Platform rejects *"Cap and Trade"* initiatives on both economic and ethical grounds. Economically, Cap and Trade will cause the cost of traditional fuels to skyrocket at a time when the economy needs to be stimulated rather than depressed. The conversion to alternative fuels simply *can't* take place fast enough or in a cost-competitive manner without *significantly* damaging the economy. Even if you delude yourself into believing it can (and if so, I've got some sunlight I'd like to sell you), it's unethical to apply Cap and Trade.

Cap and Trade works based on the premise that some fictitious *"cap"* can be placed on emissions in the name of protecting the environment. Then, rather than doing what's right for mankind, *"big business"* can pay for a *"Get Out of Jail Free"* card ... except it's not *"free."* In other words, we're going to have some *"bureaupath"* establish an upper limit (that's probably *unreasonably* low), so we can then accept what amounts to be a *bribe* to *ignore* the violation. That's a good lessen for our children. Of course, on the plus side, it certainly gives them a clearer understanding of how politics works ... or the mob for that matter. It's kind of like *"protection money."* You might expect this type of thuggish behavior from a country in which the Chairman of the Committee that establishes taxes, and the Secretary of the Department that administers the tax code fail to pay their *own* taxes, but this just *can't* happen in a *transparent* government like ours where the *"swamp has been drained"* of corrupt politicians ... as promised. That's right, isn't it?

HEALTH CARE

Speaking of bribes, that brings us to Health Care Reform. Over the past year, we've been overwhelmed with the importance of health care in the United States. I agree. Dying would just ruin my day. So, how can I stay healthy ... and afford to do it?

Health care costs have been skyrocketing for the past few decades while insurance coverage seems to have eroded. I pay a premium to mitigate the risk associated with ever increasing health care costs. The word *"premium"* implies that I'm paying *more* for the peace of mind the insurance gives me than what actuarial probability suggests the cost of the risk represents, and I'm okay with that. Heck, I pay for fire insurance and don't expect my home to burn down; I pay for automobile insurance even though history suggests that I won't have an accident; and I pay for life insurance even though I *know* that that I can never *personally* collect it. But the *cost* of health care insurance has been going *up* while the *coverage* has been going *down*.

So, I'm 100% behind the concept of improving health care insurance. I just think 2,700+ pages of legislation that reshapes one-sixth of the Nation's GDP is not the way to do it. I'm also uncomfortable with having such legislation drafted by individuals who lack the specific industry experience and sophistication that is necessary to fully understand the impact of their recommendations. While the *Party of "No"* voted against it, the *Party of "Don't Know"* drafted it … behind closed doors … and with enough earmarks to put a pig farm to shame. I thought we were promised: open debate on C-Span (which we didn't get); sufficient time to review the legislation before it would be signed into law (which we didn't get); bipartisan support (which is tough to get when one Party is excluded from participating in the drafting); no more earmarks (which we *obviously* didn't get); no more government waste (see *"earmarks"*); and no more corruption (*i.e.,* Nancy Pelosi's guarantee to *"drain the swamp"* … which we didn't get based upon the special interests that were protected within the legislation). What we *did* get was *"No Change"* in process … and *that "We Can Believe In."*

Does any *rational* human being really *believe* that the 159 new agencies that will be created by the Health Care Reform Bill will *reduce* costs? I would have supported a public option *before* I would have supported 159 new Federal agencies. The Brazilian Rain Forest will be threatened by the millions of tons of regulations that these agencies will create over the coming years; not to mention the paper that will be consumed in forms that we'll *all* have to fill out to receive health care going forward. I recommend you go *"long"* in paper mills and printing companies if this legislation doesn't get overturned.

And talk about New Useless Guys (NUGS)! The only upside to creating 159 new Federal agencies is that the tens of thousands of jobs they will create will be a less offensive way of distributing the equivalent of welfare checks: instead of a welfare check for doing *nothing*, these NUGS will receive a *paycheck*. It's the adult version of giving A's to children to make everyone feel better about themselves.

Everything in the Health Care Reform Bill costs money, and *that's* going to reduce costs ... or so we're told. At least now you know why President Obama has refused to release his college transcripts: his grades in economics, finance, and math must have been totally *underwater* (*i.e.,* well below C-level). However, we could have *actually* reduced costs had we tackled *tort* reform in the Health Care Reform Bill ... and tort reform wouldn't cost *anything*. It would simply require legislating *common sense* rules and limits to preclude or inhibit frivolous medical malpractice lawsuits and jury awards. You see, a *tremendous* amount of the cost associated with health care today is generated by physicians practicing *"defensive"* medicine.

Here's how it works. Doctors order a whole *battery* of tests for their patients that they *really don't believe* are *necessary* to *properly* diagnose and treat their patients. They order the tests *strictly* to protect themselves against frivolous law suits. You see, there may be an attorney lurking around out there who would just *love* to be able to argue that a doctor missed subjecting a patient to one *obscure* test that, subjectively, could have made a difference. Medical malpractice attorneys (like John Edwards used to be) make big bucks practicing the law this way ... and we're talking *really* big bucks!

Now, if you're the patient, you get pricked, prodded and otherwise *"violated"* because of these *"defensive"* medical practices, but your doctor really doesn't have any other choice. It's a defensive maneuver. Enter the big, bad insurance companies ... or at least we've been led to believe that they're *"big, bad insurance companies."* They're expected to cover at least a substantive portion of your medical costs, and the more tests you have, the greater the cost to them. Like any other business, they have to pass their ever increasing exposure on to the consumer ... and unfortunately, that's *you!* So, *your* insurance costs go up. Additionally, those *"big, bad insurance companies"* provide medical malpractice insurance to physicians and hospitals. When a malpractice attorney secures an unconscionably large award for his or her client in a medical malpractice lawsuit, guess who writes the check? Absolutely correct: the *"big, bad insurance company."* Guess what happens to the insurance company's cost? Right again ... they go through the roof. So, the insurance company has to pass that along to the consumer who, in this case, is *your* physician (in the form of higher medical malpractice premiums). That, in turn, raises *your* physician's cost of doing business. Now, guess who the physician has to pass along that cost increase to? You're amazing! Right again! *YOU!*

So, if a few strokes of a pen in the drafting of Health Care Reform legislation would have gone a long way toward correcting this travesty and *significantly* reducing health care costs in America (not to mention dramatically improving the efficiency with which physicians could actually *provide* health care), *why* wasn't it done? I can tell ... you're ahead of me on this one. *Politicians* would be negatively impacted!

You see, the American Trial Lawyers Association is a strong supporter of the Democratic Party; contributing almost *eight times* as much money to *Democratic* candidates as it contributes to *Republican* candidates. Throw the ACLU and its supporters into the mix and a variety of other extremely *"progressive"* legal PACs and you assure yourself that *tort* reform will *never* make it into the legislation if the majority Party has its way. Is the historic phrase *"No taxation without representation"* starting to have more meaning for you?

Was the massive Health Care Reform Bill *"necessary and proper"* under the Constitution? Probably not! Does it provide for the *"common Defense and general Welfare of the United Sates?"* Not really! So, why was it passed? The Party *in charge* thought it was *good politics*.

CSC's Platform Position: This Platform calls for the repeal of the Health Care Reform Bill and the replacement with legislature that follows our new mantra: *"Laws that Make Sense"* **(rather than** *"Laws that Make Cents"* **for political Parties); and of course** *common sense* **is presumed.**

So, after the repeal, a *single issue* **bill should be submitted and passed that addresses** *tort* **reform. Once we see how much** *that* **changes the practice of medicine and returns it to a profession rather than a** *"defensive"* **provider of services ... and how much that action reduces costs ... we will be in a position to submit and pass additional** *single issue* **legislation to systematically reduce health care costs while increasing the quality of care. Specifically:**

- **Prescription drug legislation that restricts consumer advertising. This type of advertising creates a brand preference in the mind of the general public that has nothing to a medication's efficacy. It's used to entice otherwise** *uninformed* **individuals to express a brand** *preference* **to their physician (the professional who actually** *knows* **what he or she is doing) in hopes that the physician will default to** *that* **brand to honor the patient's** request. Huge dollars are spent on this type of advertising, so you'll pick a product based upon a perception of its possible superior characteristics. For example: there's a product that warns that if you have a certain physical response *"lasting more than four hours, you should immediately go to an emergency room"* ... or any other public forum where you can *tell* everyone! I'll bet sales soared when that ad was first broadcast.

- o Guess who picks up the cost of these massive advertising campaigns? I can tell that you're way ahead of me again! So, let's just legislate them out of existence. Let the pharmaceutical companies argue the merits of their medications with *informed* decision-makers ... like your *doctor*. Your pharmaceutical costs will go down precipitously.

- Just in case you don't think this makes a difference, let's assume for a moment that the exact same medication and dosage of a particular medicine is provided to a human and an animal (let's say a donkey). The medicine for the human is likely to cost about 130% more on average than the medicine that's provided to the donkey even though everything is *exactly* the same. This is based up a Special Investigations Division report that was presented to the Committee on Government Reform, U.S. House of Representatives on February 16, 2000 (so the difference might even be greater today). The reason for *price-gouging* humans should be obvious: the pharmaceutical companies *don't incur any advertising costs* relative to donkeys ... *dumb ass* (I apologize, it was just *too* easy). Now, do you understand?

- Strangely enough, the enforcement of Immigration Law comes into play again. If an illegal alien needs medical treatment, it should be provided ... *once* in this country ... and *thereafter* in the illegal alien's country of origin. You can't live in Canada, and take advantage of it's health care system if you're not Canadian; you can't live in England, and take advantage of it's health care system if you're not British; you can't live in Mexico, and take advantage of it's

health care system if you're not Mexican. Are you detecting a trend yet?
- It's estimated that about 25% of the uncompensated costs that county hospitals incur on the southwest border result from emergency medical treatment provided to illegal aliens. Does anyone want to guess who ultimately picks up the tab?

• According to the CDC (Center for Disease Control), hospital infections are the fourth leading cause of death in the United States, behind heart disease, cancer and strokes, and about 75% of these are believed to be preventable. Here's another great opportunity for saving lives while creating jobs and eliminating welfare dependency. Hospitals would greatly benefit from more robust and diligent janitorial and sterilization services.
- This Platform calls for training and employing those interested individuals, who are currently dependent upon welfare to survive, to provide such services. It gives them new vocational opportunities that can be quickly learned and provide an invaluable service to society. The hospitals win, the patients and their families win, and the workers win (with an increased level of income and a pride in how they contribute to society). I'm fine with having the government *redirect* the welfare payments to subsidize employment costs like these for the hospitals.
- As mortality rates drop, so will the cost of treatment and, according, the cost of insurance, which ultimately translates into a reduced cost of health care. This is a classic example of how an entitlement program can be converted to provide for *"the general Welfare of the United States"* in a way that is *"necessary and proper."*

• This Platform calls for an encrypted, national health care database to be developed so that statistical analyses can be used to improve the quality and efficiency of health care while dramatically reducing costs. This is not a database of patient records but rather one constructed of information pertaining to the demonstrated effectiveness of caregivers and protocols. No information will be stored relative to a particular individual and all information will

be encrypted, so no *"privacy issue"* will exist. I actually was involved with a group that proposed this solution back in the days of the Clinton Administration (one of the members of the group participated in the development of the Apollo project for NASA, so it's not like it was just a *theoretical* model). Here's how it works:
- Treatment information is stripped of any personal identification and merged into local, regional and national databases. The reason for the subsets is to facilitate the early identification of local and regional health issues before they migrate (*i.e.*, as in the case of potential pandemics). As a result, strategies can be deployed to more effectively contain biological threats.
- Treatments are recorded and statistically tracked for efficacy. Thus, a doctor can check the database to determine which protocol / medication is *most* effective on the basis of probability. This increases the patient's chance of a quicker, more complete, and potentially more cost-effective recovery.
- The results achieved by physicians and health care facilities can be tracked (without the need to disclose patient identities) to rate their effectiveness. This can *radically* improve health care by identifying areas for recommended (or required) improvement. It also will provide a basis for *legitimately* stratifying insurable risk. As the quality of health care improves and the cost of treatments goes down, so do insurance costs and its ultimate impact on the consumer.
- As a collateral benefit, pharmaceutical companies and health care research centers will have access to data that will provide insight into development paths that offer the highest probability of success and, as a result, a better return on R&D investment both in terms of *time* and *money*.

• This Platform also calls for a comparative assessment of insurance options that consumers can understand. As they choose between providers and plans, it is difficult to develop a clear understanding of cost versus benefit. This

legislation will help consumers evaluate the cost of their insurance options versus the benefit.
- For example: most people are deluded into thinking that lower deductibles, fixed co-pays, etc. represent *better* coverage. The one thing you *can* count on is that they will carry *higher* monthly premiums. If you do the math, you may find that many of these programs are *only* favorable if you require medical attention on a fairly *regular* basis (which is not the case for most people). Instead, catastrophic health care coverage may be *far* more cost effective. With catastrophic coverage, you pay a *much* lower premium but still have extensive coverage if you have the misfortune of incurring a *serious* illness and need expensive treatment; in all of the intervening years, you've paid a much lower amount of money to the insurance company while you effectively self-insured yourself against the cost of an occasional doctor visit.
- There might even be a way to create a health care savings plan that operates like a tax-free 401K and converts to an annuity that funds catastrophic coverage when you reach your 65th birthday. It's just a matter of doing the math.

These are just a few examples of how Health Care Reform could be *responsibly* addressed with *common sense* if it wasn't used as a pawn to gain political advantage. It's unconscionable that so many politicians are willing to trade *our* health for political favors and votes. They're so enamored with *"winning"* that they take their *"eyes off the ball."* I seriously doubt that the Democrats *"want to bankrupt America"* or that Republicans just *"want you to die quickly if you get sick"* (as the two sides have said about each other). Luckily, there's a treatment for Congressmen and Senators who say such ludicrous things: it's called *losing their bid for reelection*. This Platform has gone a step further. They can't even run for consecutive terms, and their record will be tracked and published for *all* to see.

On a positive note, if the Health Care Reform Bill *isn't* repealed, it *won't* be all that bad. You see, we'll probably all get really *frustrated* with the long delays that we'll likely incur while awaiting our treatments, and the treatments themselves may become *cost prohibitive*. As a result, we'll have no option but to *stay healthy*. We'll be forced to improve our diets and increase our level of exercise. Come to think of it, this is a *brilliant* idea on the part of the Administration. No one else has been able to get us off of our couches and pry the remote controls out of our hands so that we may live healthier lives. The Health Care Reform Bill will give us *no* other option. Absolutely brilliant!

ENTITLEMENT AND RESPONSIBILITY

In the *Declaration of Independence*, Thomas Jefferson tells us that *"... all men are created equal"* and *"they are endowed by their Creator with certain unalienable Rights"* and *"that among these are Life, Liberty and the pursuit of Happiness."* Correspondingly, the *Constitution* and its Amendments provide us some specifics relative to other *unalienable* rights. Then, no less of an authority than Benjamin Franklin clarified that *"The Constitution only gives people the right to pursue happiness. You have to catch it yourself."*

Take a few moments to think about this.

We are *all* created *equal*. There is no *superior* race, religion, gender, sexual-orientation, etc.; we're all created *equal*. The *Constitution* spells out certain rights ... like freedom of religion, freedom of speech, freedom to assemble, freedom to petition for a redress of grievances against the government, etc. ... to which every citizen is *equally* entitled regardless of race, religion, gender, sexual-orientation, etc. To distinguish between groups is to deny equality ... for it *necessarily* asserts that *one* group requires *special* assistance while *another* does *not*.

That is where Franklin's quote comes into play. None of us are guaranteed *"happiness."* We are merely promised an opportunity to *"pursue"* it. If we find an excuse for *not* pursuing it, that burden is ours to bear. Sometimes it is just a reality that stands in our way. I would *love* to be a Center in the NBA (the National Basketball Association). I'm 5' 9" ... so it's probably not going to happen. That's *not* discrimination ... it's just reality. I'm not going to organize a group of frustrated basketball junkies who are my height to picket the Staples

Center. I'm not going to petition the ACLU to sue the Los Angeles Lakers for discriminating against me by refusing to let me try out. That is not a career path for which I am *qualified*. However, I still have the right to *pursue* happiness ... just in a million *other* ways.

So, we're going to address some of the greatest issues of our times in very quick fashion. They're actually pretty easy to grasp when you keep this discussion in mind and combine it with the limitation imposed upon the Federal government in Article I, Section 8 of the Constitution. Remember when we discussed how Congress is *only* allowed to collect taxes, etc. to pay for programs that *"provide for the common Defense and general Welfare of the United States"* and that all such programs must be *"necessary and proper?"* Well, those are the tests we're going to apply as we address the *"issues of the day"* in alphabetical order.

<u>Abortion</u>

Let's start with something that's *not* controversial: *abortion*. You can euphemistically refer to it as *Pro-Choice*, but in the end, the issue is abortion. On the other hand, *Right-to-Life* is a bit of a euphemism too. It asserts a right: a right for *others* to make a decision for *you*. There are no *"winners"* on this issue.

 **CSC's Platform Position:** This Platform shall permit people to make their own personal decisions. The reality is that they will *regardless* of what the law says.

Abortion was illegal when I was a child, and yet it was carried out behind closed doors and in dark alleys, with great emotional and physical risk. With legalization came a reduction of danger. Did it become a bit *too* easy to procure? Probably. Did proponents *underestimate* and *understate* the *emotional trauma* associated with the choice? Perhaps. Did they *understate* the *importance* of the decision and make it appear to be just another form of birth control? Almost definitely. So, why allow it to continue?

Having a child should be a *conscious* decision. Creating a life should not be an accident for which the *child* is potentially punished. Those who have to make the decision are sentenced to carry the burden of their decision with them for the rest of their lives. There are no guarantees when it comes to *"life."* Each live birth could give rise to the next Gandhi ... or the next Hitler. Let's trust God to provide people with the guidance they need to make the right decision and accept the fact that whatever that decision might be ... it is what was meant to be. The reality is that whatever happens is likely to have happened with or without the government's approval. So, at least, let's try to make it safe.

Does this position provide for *"the general Welfare of the United States?"* Yes. It addresses an issue that potentially impacts *every* citizen in one way or another. It *preserves* the rights of those who would *not* consider abortion as an alternative under *any* set of circumstances. It *preserves* the rights of those who would *only* consider abortion as an alternative under an *extremely* limited set of circumstances (such as a rape or a risk to the mental or physical health of the mother). It also *preserves* the rights of those who would just consider abortion as an *alternative;* nothing more and nothing less. Hopefully, social folkways and mores can be taught to reduce the latter group of people to a *very* small minority so that abortion will be viewed as a *last* resort. *Responsibility* and *respect* need to be taught at an *early* age; more so than sex education, which can be deferred until pubescent change dictates its attention.

Is this position *"necessary and proper?"* Yes. The issue isn't going to go away. It needs to be addressed ... and in a compassionate, thoughtful, and equitable way that embraces the reality that *individuals* will make their *own* decisions. Ignoring the problem won't make it go away, so the option is to either legislate to permit the choice to be made *legally* ... or condemn it to be made *illegally*. In the absence of King Solomon, we need to abdicate the decision to divide the baby in half.

This Platform also recommends that serious deliberations be held to determine what *reasonable* limitations may be imposed. Great consideration should be given to the age of the woman who is bearing the child, the rights of the man who shared in the act of conception, the period of time in which the decision must be made before the rights of the mother (absent extenuating circumstances) give way to the rights of the developing fetus. Secular, therapeutic counseling should be incorporated into the decision-making process to assure that the parties involved are *fully* aware of the breadth and depth of the choice they are about to make (either way); and educational programs concerning contraception methods (*i.e.,* what, how and why) should be provided to those in need. And may we learn to *accept* that whatever choice those individuals make represents what is *supposed* to be.

Affirmative Action

CSC's Platform Position: This Platform calls for an elimination of the concept of Affirmative Action. Affirmative Action is a particularly insidious form of discrimination and necessarily suggests that one group of individuals isn't *"created equal"* and needs special assistance to *"pursue happiness."* That does nothing but deepen the misplaced prejudicial beliefs of all parties involved.

For example: let's return to my basketball reference and assume I want to play Center in the NBA. Chuck Hayes is the shortest Center in the *history* of the NBA at 6'6". Most of the Centers are *at least* 7' tall and can probably *reach* higher than I can *jump*. I can make a strong argument that I am being discriminated against because of my height. League officials will argue that I simply *can't compete* because of my height (not to mention my general lack of ability and that I fall into a *"suspect age category"* – which is yet *another* possible grounds for bringing a discrimination lawsuit).

But wait! What if the Federal government were to *mandate* that a certain number of 5'9 individuals be allowed to play Center in the league (or even be required on the roster of each team)? Establishing a quota, if you will. *"Ridiculous,"* you say. Why? Again, you reiterate what the league officials say; the fact that I *can't compete*. Well, what if you made special accommodations for my being 5'9"? You know, like any team that plays me gets 20 points per game and 15 rebounds (at the time of their choice). *Now*, we're *leveling* the playing field!

But, is this fair to some 7' Center who can actually *play* but gets *cut* because the team has to carry me on its roster? Will the other Centers in the league accept me as an *equal*, since I'll probably *post* numbers that are comparable to theirs (no pun intended for you basketball aficionados) ... or will they look at me as somebody who *only* got to where I am because I received preferential treatment; thus, *deepening* their prejudice against people who are 5'9".

Sure, the example is absurd ... but you've got to admit, it conjures up a pretty funny visual. However, it's really *not* as unfair as Affirmative Action. You see, in the example, I had a *physical* limitation that *prevented* me from competing. I wasn't 7' tall. So, what if I *was* 7' tall and was a decent natural athlete, but I either just hadn't *applied* myself ... or I *hadn't* had the benefit of good coaching and competition, parental support, personal confidence, or any of the myriad of other reasons that prevented me from being competitive. What if I was White (you know the old wives' tale) or, perhaps, a Native American and my tribe didn't embrace basketball in its culture? What if my religion didn't allow me to play on the Sabbath, and the NBA scheduled games on every day that ends in Y? What if I was a woman and the NBA said there was a separate league for women (the WNBA)? What if I had a non-traditional sexual-orientation and liked to cross-dress? Oh wait, forget that one ... Dennis Rodman already broke that barrier!

The reality is that Affirmative Action is a concept that is *deeply* steeped with *societal bias*. It gives *"points and rebounds"* to individuals on a basis of their minority status. It *assumes* that they either just hadn't *applied* themselves or they *hadn't* had the benefit of coaching and competition, parent support, personal confidence, or any of the myriad of other reasons that society assigns to their *stereotype* to justify its presumption that they are otherwise not competitive (does this argument sound familiar). It assumes that they *need* assistance to compete simply because of their minority status.

I don't care if we give them an advantage because of their race, religion, gender, sexual-orientation or any other characteristic. As soon as we do, we are *by definition* discriminating against anyone who competes with them. That is *demeaning* to the individuals who received the assistance, it is unfair to those who are negatively affected, and it perpetuates prejudicial myths.

In the first instance, it suggests that they can't compete on their own merits. In the second instance, it potentially fosters resentment among those *against* whom the playing field is tilted. In the third (*i.e.,* circumstances in which the benefactors' skill sets *are inadequate* to compete *"once they're in the game"*), it only serves to *reinforce* misperceptions about the minority as a whole.

So, does the law provide for *"the general Welfare of the United States?"* No. It provides a brief competitive advantage to a small segment of society regardless of whether they need it. I have a feeling that President Obama is an *inherently* bright individual and wouldn't need any of us to *"spot him points"* ... on a test or a basketball court. In fact, I think he'd *resent* it. And if you competed head-to-head with him and he only won because you *"spotted him points,"* I rather seriously doubt that *he* would *accept* the win any more than *you* would *accept* the loss.

Next question: is the law *"necessary and proper?"* No. It is obviously *not "necessary"* nor is it even *"proper."* Its failure on the first point is obvious. Its failure on the second stems from the fact that it *creates* discrimination to *eliminate* discrimination, and that's absurd. We need to *cure* the cancer rather than putting a *band-aid* on it.

A good starting point is to begin to teach people that we truly *are* all *"created equal"* ... not *identical* ... but *equal* in our ability to *pursue happiness*. I'm 5'9" and Shaquille O'Neal is 7'1". We're *not* identical, but we *both* have the freedom to pursue happiness. So, repeat after me:

- Children with good parents, bad parents, and no parents can grow up to be successful.

- Children from the inner-city, the suburbs, and rural America can grow up to be successful.
- Children who attend good schools and bad schools can grow up to be successful.
- Children of any race can grow up to be successful.
- Children of deep faith, moderate faith, and no faith at all can grow up to be successful.
- Children of either sex and any sexual-orientation can grow up to be successful.
- And children of any combination of the above can grow up to be successful.
- Children who attend public schools, private schools or home schools can grow up to be successful.

Let's stop telling them that they *can't* ... either directly or through programs like Affirmative Action that *imply* that they can't. Let's fix what's broken rather than masking the symptoms. It may take a generation or two, but we can do this!

<u>Charity</u>

CSC's Platform Position: This Platform has already called for a Flat Tax and the elimination of *all* tax deductions to simplify the tax code and eliminate abuses. In that regard, the charitable deduction will be eliminated.

I believe this will have a collateral benefit in that, over time, people will begin to *reconnect* with charity in a deeper and more meaningful way. Many people write a check today because it's easier than getting involved; besides they you get a deduction on their taxes. What could be better? The answer is simple: giving your *time* is better. It's better for the charity that you are assisting, and it's better for you and those around you.

Charities can't *raise* enough money to pay for the benefits they would receive if every donor would give their *time* as well as their money. The impact on the charities would be enormous. Let's look at Habitat for Humanity as an example.
- Habitat for Humanity recruits corporate sponsors that help defray the cost of materials, supplies, and tools. But

those corporate sponsors also recruit employees to help build the home. With enough *people* and a *limited* number of tools, Habitat for Humanity can build a house. With enough money for all the tools in the world but with no *people* to help, the home would *never* get built. If you want to make a difference, give your *time*.

I'll be the first to admit that it's not nearly as easy to give your time as it is to just write a check. The check only takes a few seconds, and it only creates a minor economic inconvenience. Unfortunately, the sense of fulfillment is equally fleeting. Having been very active in charities (including Habitat for Humanity), I can assure you that while giving your time is a much greater imposition (it *can* be *extremely* inconvenient), *nothing* can come *close* to the sense of pride and community you will feel at the end of your service. Time is the most precious gift that we have, and our character can best be judged by how unselfishly we use it.

Entitlement Programs

 **CSC's Platform Position:** This Platform adheres to the concept that *"all men are created equal, that they are endowed ... with certain unalienable Rights, that among these are Life, Liberty and the pursuit of Happiness."* We are not *guaranteed* "Happiness" nor are we *entitled* to it. We just have the right to *pursue* it.

One of the greatest risks to our society these days is the sense of *"entitlement"* that has spread like a cancer. I cringe when I hear the phrase *"I'm entitled to ..."* because it generally represents a misplaced and self-defeating belief. Generally speaking, the people uttering the phrase aren't even remotely *entitled* to what they've been led to *believe* is *theirs*.

"Entitlement" is a drug that can make us *every* bit as *lethargic* as the most powerful narcotic you can imagine. It is even more dangerous because we may not even be aware that we are *"taking"* it. It is administered to us in political speeches, in media broadcasts, in articles we read, and in our daily interaction with others who are already addicted. And before we

know it, we're addicted too. We're addicted to expecting the *government* to care for us; we're addicted to believing that *"others"* are to blame for the path we have chosen; we're addicted to demanding that *"they"* pay for *our* needs; and, in the end, we are addicted to believing that we are *"entitled."*

The word *"entitled"* is defined as *"to give title to ... or to furnish with a right or claim to something."* The only things you're *"entitled to"* are: the opportunity to compete on a level playing field for what you want; and the opportunity to receive what you have been promised for that which you have paid (either with effort, money, in trade, or by vote). Anything beyond that is inconsistent with the *Declaration of Independence* and the *Constitution* and its Amendments.

With respect to government programs:

- You are *entitled* to receive the services for which your tax dollars were collected.
    - You are entitled to the freedoms guaranteed by the *Constitution* and its Amendments.
    - You are *entitled* to be defended by the United States government.
    - You are *entitled* to have the opportunity to access government programs that are developed to serve *all* citizens in their pursuit of *"Life, Liberty and ... Happiness."*
    - You are *entitled* to receive Medicare, Social Security, Unemployment, Workers' Compensation and other programs to the degree that you have contributed if they are applicable to your circumstances. If you have not contributed ... you are not *"entitled."*
- In turn, the government has an *obligation* to protect and preserve the Republic and to honor its promises with regard to the purposes for which your tax dollars were collected.
- The government has *no* obligation to provide you with a job or any other type of economic support unless you are incapable of caring for yourself and have become a *"ward of the State."*

This Platform believes that if the government makes an accommodation to provide you with compensation or services that are otherwise not offered to *all* citizens (*i.e.*, for *"the general Welfare of the United States"*), and from a fund to which you have not contributed, you shall have the responsibility to perform community service in return. This could be something as simple as helping to clean up America by picking up litter from the side of the road for a specific number of days a month to something far more complex (perhaps serving a government agency in a capacity for which you have a unique skill). Bottom line: *you* have to *contribute* to your country.

President Kennedy had it right when he said, *"Ask not what your country can do for you. Ask what you can do for your country."* Over the past several decades, we have moved too far away from this sense of obligation. We have been *seduced* by the lure of political promises. We think the government is a *"free store"* from which we can expect to receive our essentials without having to balance the ledgers. As a result, many of us have traded our *pride* for an *apathetic* existence that *shifts* the burden of our care to *others*. It's time to wake up. So, repeat after me:

- I am *proud*.
- I am *worthwhile*.
- I don't *need* someone *else* to provide for me.
- I will *work* to achieve what I desire in life.
- I will *pay back* those who help me along the way, either directly or through demonstrating that I have become *all* that *they* hoped I could be.
- I owe my country, my family, and myself my *best* effort.
- In return, my country owes me a safe environment within which to live and the opportunity to *"pursue happiness"* without false limitations.

It may take a generation or two to evolve from the state of dependency we have unfortunately embraced, but it can be done. The journey begins today.

The Justice System

CSC's Platform Position: The Justice System may not be *completely* broken, but it's running *"rough"* and needs a significant tune-up. In surrendering to *"political correctness,"* it appears that the Department of Justice now only selectively enforces the law. For example: some cities can flaunt Federal immigration laws without fear of reprimand, while others are sued for trying to enforce it; Congressional leadership and Cabinet members who create and administer the tax code, respectively, may fail to pay taxes without being subjected to the same treatment that *"Main Street"* citizens have come to expect; and voter intimidation at the polls, which were once *"hallowed grounds,"* no longer merits outrage as an assault on one of our most cherished rights.

The courts have become backlogged to the degree that a citizen's Sixth Amendment right to a *"speedy trial"* is almost a thing of the past; and overcrowded jails have become an excuse for ignoring the Court's best judgment when it comes to sentencing. The appellate process has eroded into just another *"back hole"* into which taxpayer money disappears; and civil trials have become less and less *"civil."*

Our three-tier system of justice remains; only, it no longer just defines a lower court, an appellate court, and a court of last resort. Today, it also reflects a set of rules for celebrities and politicians, a set of rules for those who can afford to participate, and a set of rules for the rest of us. It is equally disturbing that we have become so preoccupied with making sure that the Defendants' rights are protected that we have increasing secured *that* ideal by *sacrificing* the rights of the victims. *Enough!*

This Platform calls for *one* set of laws ... *equally applied.* The *Constitution* doesn't provide for laws to be established that treat *one* group of citizens differently than *another*. It doesn't afford superior rights to those who are *not* citizens, nor does it favor the rights of the convicted over the rights of those citizens who *abide* by the law. Let's get back to the basics.

Speaking of which, we spend an inordinate amount of time and money litigating and prosecuting issues that are tied to social *folkways*. This Platform calls for the law to focus on issues of social *mores*. For clarification: *"folkways"* are social conventions that are not considered to be *"morally significant"* by society in general (based upon behavior and acceptance); *"mores"* are social conventions that are generally regarded as *essential* for the maintenance of society and the violation of which merits harsh negative consequences. As an example: the sale and use of alcoholic beverages was rendered illegal by the Eighteenth Amendment in 1919. Unfortunately, it appears that drinking was viewed as a *folkway* rather than something that ascended to the level of social *mores*, and as a result, its use *continued* with disregard to the law. The ongoing behavior was so prevalent that it forced the repeal of the Eighteenth Amendment in 1933 via the Twenty-First Amendment. Name your vice, and you'll see something similar.

Hard drugs (heroin, opium, cocaine, etc.) are illegal. Bayer (now, famous for its aspirin) stopped selling *heroin* in 1913. Then in 1914, the government passed the Harrison Narcotics Tax Act to *regulate* and *tax* it (along with opium and cocaine). It wasn't until 1924 (or 5 years *after* alcohol had been banned), that the government *outlawed* heroin (along with opium and cocaine). Today, it contributes significantly to our illegal immigration problem and represents about a $60 billion untaxed *"industry"* in the United States. From a personal perspective, I don't do drugs; so, I *really* don't care if they're legal or not. However, a logical argument can be made for decriminalization (similar to the issue with alcohol). Here's my one condition: if the use of drugs (or any other vice) leads one to violate social *mores* (*i.e.*, causing threat or bodily harm to another individual, destruction or theft of property, etc.), then the *punishment* should be harsh enough to *"capture the attention"* of potential violators and *"dissuade"* them from such action: no *"slap on the wrist"* for first-time offenders; no community service; we're talking straight jail time ... *fully* served. Remember my discussion of *"cruel and unusual punishment"* under the Eighth Amendment? Well, I haven't had a change in mind. Will this *eliminate* the problem? No. Will it *mitigate* the problem? I think so.

I could discuss the application of this same approach to prostitution, but I would have to name too many public officials. And I could discuss it with regard to illegal gambling, but no one would pay any attention because they're too busy picking their lottery numbers and revealing the *"scratch-offs"* on the game tickets they bought from the *State*. Suffice it to say, the argument is the same.

People like me *aren't* going to manifest a change in behavior if these things are legalized, and those who are currently ignoring the law aren't going to change their behavior either. Those in the middle might be tempted to explore their new-found options, but they would have a clear understanding of the *significant* risk they would be taking by surrendering to temptation. It might even benefit society by instilling a greater sense of *personal* responsibility. Additionally, law enforcement would be able to truly focus on defending our safety, and the often violent criminal behavior associated with such issues might be dramatically reduced or even eliminated.

To further reduce the *"crowding of the docket"* that results in long delays and additional costs with respect to civil suits and criminal prosecutions, this Platform calls for a shift in the appellate process. There are foreign countries that have an interesting approach that has applicability to our justice system as well. You retain the right to appeal; it's just subject to a few *"conditions."* I like to call the conditions: *"Double or Nothing."*

- Let's say you lose in the lower court and face 5 years in jail and a $25,000 fine. You can appeal. If you win on appeal, you go free and pay nothing. If you lose on appeal but made a strong argument, you still have to serve the 5 years and pay the $25,000 fine. However, if you *waste* the Court's time (and the taxpayers' money ... or your own) by filing a frivolous appeal, you *now* get to serve 10 years and pay a fine of $50,000. Want to try again? Go for it! You'll be looking at 20 years in jail and a $100,000 fine. It takes all the fun out of filing frivolous appeals just because you can.

I'm willing to bet that this will help clear the docket and stop the hundreds of millions of taxpayers' dollars that are wasted on baseless appeals each year.

Another area of opportunity ties back to this Platform's position on the enforcement of Immigration Laws. It is estimated that illegal aliens comprise approximately 3 percent of this Nation's general population. Yet, they comprise about 17 percent of our Nation's prison population at an annual cost of about $8-9 billion (just for incarceration). Dealing with illegal immigration according to the laws that are currently on the books would:

- *Reduce* the overall amount of crime in the United States (and the associated victims' suffering);
- *Reduce* the crowding of court dockets;
- *Reduce* overcrowding in our State and Federal prisons, which results in early release for many offenders; and
- *Reduce* the overall cost of the justice system (from law enforcement ... to court time and legal representation ... to prison facilities, maintenance and staffing ... to the feeding, clothing and care of the prisoners).

And finally, this Platform has already discussed *tort reform* in the area of Health Care Reform. Suffice it to say that similar opportunities exist within other specific areas of the practice of law. This Platform will leave those to your imagination now that the thought process has been started.

Racism

CSC's Platform Position: Today, it's *"politically correct"* to create a *"Sanctuary City"* that serves as a haven for illegal immigrants. But if you support the enforcement of Federal Immigration Law, you're a *racist*. Of course, you're also a *racist* if you exercise your right to *"peaceably ... assemble, and to petition the government for a redress of grievances"* ... at least, you are if you do it at a Tea Party rally as opposed to ... say ... an NAACP convention. It's actually fairly easy to become a *racist* in our *"politically correct"* world. Once again, it's fun to *"channel"* Jeff Foxworthy's *"redneck"* comedy in this regard:

- If you think English should be a required language ... you might be a *racist*.
- If you think that people who can't afford a home should rent rather than be given loans upon which they almost assuredly will default ... you might be a *racist*.
- If you think that building a Mosque near the site where the World Trade once stood and scheduling its proposed 2011 opening on September 11th might be akin to opening a Ku Klux Klan Meeting Hall next to a memorial for Martin Luther King, Jr. on the national holiday named in his honor ... you might be a *racist*.
- If you disagree with our President over *anything* ... you might be a *racist* ... or at least you might be a racist *half* of the time. The other *half*, you're probably just guilty of sedition.

We live in a world in which *segregated* groups routinely call *integrated* groups *"racist,"* if the segregated group doesn't like the integrated group's message. Interestingly enough, the term *"racist"* cannot only be used to *attack* an individual's or group's *behavior*, it has disintegrated to the point that it is now used to *defend* biased behavior. For example: those who complained about *racially-directed* voter intimidation were criticized for being *racially* motivated since their complaint was directed against individual members of a *racially-biased* organization. And while Shirley Sherrod was inappropriately *"thrown under the bus"* for remarks that were taken out of context, the reaction of the audience itself, which was comprised of members of an organization that had just accused a *far* more homogeneous group of being racially insensitive, was ... well, *racially insensitive*.

In the Preamble to this Platform, I cited Dr. Martin Luther King, Jr.'s famous speech *"I Have A Dream"* (see AMEN ... AMEN). This Platform calls for everyone to revisit that speech and drink from the same fountain of that dream. While it acknowledged racial injustice as it existed at that time, it wasn't a dream that only touched upon *racial* equality. It was a dream of equality ... *period!*

Early in his speech, Dr. King provides:

"In a sense we have come to our nation's capital to cash a check. When the architects of our republic wrote the magnificent words of the Constitution and the Declaration of Independence, they were signing a promissory note to which every American was to fall heir. This note was a promise that all men, yes, black men as well as white men, would be guaranteed the unalienable rights of life, liberty, and the pursuit of happiness."

We have lost sight of his vision. Luckily, we need only look to the end of his speech for direction:

"From every mountainside, let freedom ring. And when this happens, when we allow freedom to ring, when we let it ring from every village and every hamlet, from every state and every city, we will be able to speed up that day when all of God's children, black men and white men, Jews and Gentiles, Protestants and Catholics, will be able to join hands and sing in the words of the old Negro spiritual, 'Free at last! Free at last! Thank God Almighty, we are free at last!'"

Racism isn't a really a *racial* issue ... it's an issue of *equality*: an *equal* opportunity to be *safe* in our *lives* and *liberties* and to *pursue happiness*; nothing *more* ... and nothing *less*. It cannot be allowed to continue to be used as a tool with which to *isolate* one race from another; to *provide* benefits beyond an *equal* opportunity that may otherwise *engender* resentment and *solidify* false stereotypes; and to *stifle* legitimate communication. The "R" word should be as offensive as the "N" word is when it is uttered. Dr. King didn't limit his comments to *"black men and white men."* He expanded his discussion to *"Jews and Gentiles, Protestants and Catholics."* He understood the breadth of the issue.

This Platform's position is simple: stop the *divisive* accusations of *racism* that are made just to further one's *own* cause at the expense of *another's*, and do not apply *generic* accusations to reflect upon the integrity of an *individual* unless the facts irrefutably support that position. For example: it is factually inaccurate and patently unfair to state that *"there are racists within the Tea Party"* and *"therefore, all members of the Tea Party are racists."* Probability asserts that the *premise* is almost undoubtedly true (*i.e., "there are racists within the Tea Party"… as there are in the Democratic and Republican Parties as well*), but the conclusion does not necessarily follow (*i.e.,* that *"all members of the Tea Party are racists"*). There are racists of some kind in almost *any* collection of individuals, but that *cannot* serve as an indictment against *all* members of the group *unless* the group's membership requirements exclusively require it. It's a bit of a sliding scale. For example: there undoubtedly have been racists among Catholics … but Mother Teresa almost assuredly was *not* one of them (as can be said for the vast majority of Catholics). Conversely, the Ku Klux Klan has historically endorsed racial supremacy, and the conclusion that its members embrace that belief is clearly more sustainable. A group like the National Association for the Advancement of Colored People (the NAACP) is likely to fall somewhere in between those extremes since its focus is somewhat linear from a racial perspective and a vocal group within its membership has demonstrated a tendency to be quick to judge *"outsiders"* whose views may differ.

When it comes to *"racism,"* there is a Latin phrase that comes to mind: *"res ipsa loquitur"* … which translates to *"the thing speaks for itself."* In my experience, those who shout *"racism"* the loudest and most frequently would be well-served to take *personal* inventories; either that, or be prepared to accept the consequences of building their glass houses next to a rock quarry. For the rest of us, we probably recognize *"racism"* when we see it (sort of like when Supreme Court Justice, Potter Stewart, stated that hard-core pornography was *"hard to define,"* but "*I know it when I see it*").

In that regard, this Platform suggests that you follow standard military protocol when it comes to engaging an enemy: *Identify, Isolate* and *Defeat. Identifying* racism is usually easy. *Isolating* it may be enough to defeat it over time; but if more is needed, please have the courage to address the issue. Otherwise, your silent *acquiescence* is, effectively, your *accep-*

tance. In the end, *your* freedom is every bit as at stake as the freedom of those whom you defend. When you allow *one* segment of society to lose *its* freedom, it's only a matter of time before you'll lose your *own*.

Same-Sex Marriage

 **CSC's Platform Position:** I've already addressed *"same-sex marriage"* to some degree in the Section in which I eliminated *"political correctness"* (see AMEN ... AMEN). However, it's prominent enough to merit individual attention. And please note: I am *not* using the term *"same-sex marriage"* to be *"politically correct."* I simply think it's more *accurate* than the term *"gay marriage."* Not *all* marriages are *gay*. In fact, some are quite *unhappy*.

Unless someone can prove that a single religion's interpretation of the world is correct and get everyone else's buy-in, let's take religion out of the equation. Upon that basis, this Platform will provide for the marriage of two *unrelated* people ... without any further reservation other than that they *love* each other. Who are we to judge other people's feelings? Some people love each other deeply, and their marriages fail. Others appear to view each other with contempt, and their marriages stand the test of time. Bottom line: we are all *"created equal,"* and we are all guaranteed the opportunity to *"pursue happiness."* As Robert Browning once wrote ...

"It doesn't matter who you love, or how you love, but that you love."

Now, I *do* draw a line in that sand: one of the parties may *not* be a farm animal ... no matter *how* cute the farm animal is. But two humans ... of the opposite sex, same sex, same race, different race, same religion, different religion ... I don't care; I'm okay with it because it's none of my business.

Truth be told, it's really none of the government's business either. It's almost certainly none of the *Federal* government's business, and it probably shouldn't be any of the *State* government's business unless children are involved. Here's the way it should work.

Two adults get married. At some point, one (or both of them) decides to leave the relationship. This Platform says:
- Take what you had when you *entered* the relationship;
- Split up everything you acquired *during* the relationship equally;
- Then, shake hands and go your separate ways.

Here's the reality: *"Dissolution"* is a euphemism for *"Divorce,"* and there is almost no such thing as *"No Fault."* So, if one or both of you feel a compelling need to discontinue the marriage, you *both* need to take responsibility for your own lives. You came into this world with nothing, and you're only promised an *equal* opportunity to *"pursue happiness." "Life after separation"* should not create an exception to the Thirteenth Amendment, which was supposed to abolish slavery.

If children are involved, all bets are off. The courts *must* become involved to protect the best interests of the children. That intervention provides for *"the general Welfare of the United States"* and is both *"necessary and proper"* to protect the children.

Now, this Platform is *really* going to *"go rogue"* and suggest that other than presiding over *"the best interests of the children,"* the government has *no* other role in marriage. Marriage has just become a way to assert State authority and raise money through licensing fees and taxes. It also provides some pretty heavy-duty legal work and keeps the Domestic Relations division of your local court quite busy. The fact that State Legislatures have become so prescriptive of what a spouse is *"entitled to"* in a Divorce or Dissolution has, in my opinion, *contributed* to the *increase* in the divorce rate. Whenever a party begins to believe they're *entitled* to something in the future without providing any mutual consideration in return, multiple elements of the *Seven Deadly Sins* rear their ugly heads and nothing good ever becomes of the situation. So, anger and bitter vindictiveness intrude where love once ruled. Let the hand of God marry you or, if you don't belief in God, let your belief in each other join you together in matrimony. If you can refrain from allowing *matrimony* to evolve into a form of *martyr-money*, you'll probably do just fine.

On a historical note: marriage evolved as an element of personal property law under which women were *chattel* owned by men. It was apparently necessary at the time to suppress the number of bar fights that would otherwise arise over to whom a particular woman might belong ... and when you're drunk, your mind tends to play tricks on you. Remember: this was also back in the day when men could beat their wives ... but only with a switch no bigger in circumference than their thumb. And for those Black history buffs out there who like to point out that the *"racist"* Framers only allowed a slave to count as three-fifths of person (relative to apportionment), please note that Black *men* were specifically given the right to *vote* in 1870 through the Fifteenth Amendment, while *all* women had to wait *another* 50 years until the Nineteenth Amendment was passed to give them the *same* right to vote. So, you're probably going to have to wait in line if you think that reparations are in order. The *women* of this country will be standing in front of you.

In any event, the pendulum has swung, and Domestic Relations law now somewhat favors women. In same-sex marriages, the questions become:
- *How will the body-of-law respond to the inevitable break-ups of same-sex marriages?*
- *How will spousal benefits be impacted at the business level?*
- *How will the tax code treat same-sex unions?*
- *Etc., etc., etc.*

EDUCATION

I withheld *"Education"* until the very end of this Platform. That means, unlike the Democratic and Republican Party Platforms, I am not going to spend the last few moments of our time together pandering to special interests in an attempt to get votes. Remember: I am the *Common Sense Czar*, and I do not *need* anyone's vote!

With all due respect to Puerto Rico, Guam, American Samoa, the Northern Mariana Islands, and the U.S. Virgin Islands, your admissions as States are on hold until we clean up our own act (their statehood was the last issue addressed by the *DNC's Platform*). Adding additional complexity to a situation we have already proven incompetent to address will only add to our problems at this time. So, hang tight! If and when we do consider your countries for statehood, we'll be in much better shape.

And as for all you Native Americans out there, including Alaska Natives and Native Hawaiians, (the last group addressed by the *RNC's Platform*), you're citizens of the United States. If this Platform is successful in restoring the Republic and honoring your *"unalienable rights"* of *"life, liberty, and the pursuit of happiness,"* everything should be cool!

As a result, I'm going to address what I consider to be our best hope for *"Change We Can Believe In"* ... a *return* to the *Republic* ... for which our flag stands. In my opinion, that will require generational change; and generational change will require a concerted investment in the education of our citizens, both young and old.

CSC's Platform Position: This Platform calls for a reform of our Educational system. For adults, much of the change will come from prior Platform positions that provide reasonable assurances that our Nation's leadership will improve over time. When that transformation begins to occur, we will begin to experience an immediate and refreshing change. Our representatives will no longer have a need to continually campaign. They will be able to focus on the jobs we have elected them to do. All the false promises, fake smiles, and phony handshakes will fade away ... giving way to the *truth*. As we begin to enjoy this new experience of hearing the truth, we'll become better at discerning it.

For example: While I find Press Secretary Gibbs (whom I affectionately refer to as Press Secretary *"Glib"*) to be *wildly* entertaining as he disingenuously tries to cover the tracks of various political officials, I couldn't help feeling sorry for him when he made the almost inexcusable *faux pas* of telling the *truth* during the Summer of 2010.

First, he said the Democrats were *"at risk"* of losing the House of Representatives in the November election. Now, you'd have to be living on a different *planet* not to acknowledge that this was indeed a possibility ... or you'd have to be Nancy Pelosi ... but then, I repeat myself. The Speaker verbally assaulted Press Secretary *"Glib"* for even *suggesting* the possibility of that occurrence ... to the point that I'm sure he could only dream about being able to steal her *ruby slippers* if the House were to ever fall down upon her.

Then, Press Secretary *"Glib"* admitted that the White House "*acted without knowing all the facts*" when it responded to the video clip of Shirley Sherrod presenting at an NAACP meeting. The White House and United States Department of Agriculture ignored the actual *intent* of the clip (*i.e.,* the audience's initial supportive reaction to what sounded like reverse discrimination) and came down hard on Ms. Sherrod without listening to the rest of her story. Luckily, in *other* facets of Executive power, *two* parties have to *confirm* the code before the missiles are launched. In any event, it was actually quite *refreshing* (not to mention a bit *shocking*), to hear the Press Secretary step up and *tell the truth* on *two* ... count them ... *two* occasions ... almost back-to-back. Expect him to be asked to step down shortly. We can't have that type of behavior in the White House ... until *this* Platform is in full force. *Then*, you'd *better* get used to it.

The real focus of this Platform's Educational Program is on reforming the system that addresses the needs of our children. Until we begin to re-empower parents with the belief that they have the *ability* and *responsibility* to provide guidance to their children, I'm leaving nothing to chance. Our current educational system is *broken*. We'll spend about $1 *trillion* of taxpayers' money on education in the United States during 2010. Is anyone other than me *unimpressed* with the return we're getting on our investment? Test scores show that our elementary school children are performing poorly compared to international standards, our middle school students are even worse, and our high school students are essentially *unable* to compete. It is even more frightening that revisionist history and *"no fail"* policies have *politicized* the educational process in the United States. We are, in effect, *sacrificing* our future.

We also suffer from a declining population base as compared to other parts of the world. Fact: India has more *honor students* than we have *students*. How does that bode for maintaining technological superiority going forward?

Strangely enough, a lot of the problems that have been *caused* by politics can be *corrected* through political initiatives. Applying this Platform's political candidate standards will be a giant first step. With better representatives serving *the People*, better ideas will result. But to assure that this continues to be the case, we also need to revamp the educational system to help children learn how to distinguish right from wrong. That will address a myriad of problems over time; from creating a fiscally and socially responsible return to the Republic ... to eliminating social injustices such as racism, sexism, etc. Our future generations will simply be too *"street wise"* to be as easily duped as our recent generations have been. The real key to educational reform is to concentrate on the best interests of the students.

Let's start at the core: the teachers. There's an age-old saying that *"Those who can, do. Those who can't, teach."* There is a degree of truth to this adage, just as there is to its corollary: *"Those who can't teach ... go into politics."* This Platform calls for several changes to improve the educational system's ability to serve the *best interests of the students:*

- Teachers should be required to have experience; not only *teaching* experience, but *real world* experience.
  - Many of today's teachers enter the teaching profession *directly* out of college. They have limited if *any* real world experience. As a result, their beliefs have been greatly influenced by what *their* teachers *taught* them. They may not have the experience to question whether *their* teachers' beliefs were valid in the first instance. Thus, fallacious reasoning can be perpetuated over generations; embedding the beliefs even more deeply, from one to the next.

- Requiring a *"residency"* (much like the medical profession) would allow teachers to *"test"* whether the *theoretical* concepts they learned in college are in alignment with *practical* applications within the *real* world. This would clearly serve the *best interests of the students* while subliminally reinforcing the importance of questioning *"theory"* from the teacher's perspective. There is an additional texture that can be communicated from personal experiences, and the students will sense that difference and assign a higher level of credibility to the lesson. Analogously, mothers can give a better description of what it's like to give birth than men who have read a book about it; and people with extensive leadership experience are probably better suited to understand the challenges of similar roles than ... say ... community organizers.
- As it did relative to politicians, combat troops, law enforcement officers, and first responders (like firefighters) earlier, this Platform suggests that teachers need to be *paid* more to attract better (and more experienced) talent.
  - Current levels of compensation preclude many individuals from choosing teaching as a preferred career path. While it's nice to *theoretically* believe that *dedication* to teaching should be enough ... in the *real world*, it isn't.
  - This might also require a break from the current union environment. Teachers' unions have become *very* powerful political forces, which should *not* be their primary objective. Union environments also tend to engender *mediocrity* rather than supporting the *meritocracy* that is vital to serving the best interest of the students. Compensation should *not* be aligned with seniority. It should be awarded to those teachers who *demonstrate* the ability to help students *excel*. Again, the test should always be: what is in the *best interests of the students* ... rather than what is in the best interests of the union?
- If the federal government is going to spend a certain number of tax dollars per student, parents should be allowed to

decide if those dollars will be used to pay for a public education or repurposed to pay part of a private school's tuition or to offset the cost of home schooling (via a school voucher program or some form of dependent tax relief).
- o Why should students in a *free* country be *compelled* to attend a public school? That archaic approach *precludes* competition and *suppresses* improvement. In some cases, it effectively precludes families from having a choice, which is the equivalent to a State-run monopoly. It also creates even more damage when the public school environment drifts away from discipline and achievement to an environment of anarchy and *"everyone passes"* so as not to bruise anyone's psyche. Is it any wonder that our public school graduates are generally non-competitive when compared to their international peers?
- I'm not so naïve as to allow a voucher program to be applied to home schooling unless a verification process is also in place. I have seen the Welfare System abused for years, and I have no reason to doubt that there would be a raft of individuals *"home schooling"* their children in name only. Therefore, this Platform would institute verification procedures such as unscheduled, on-site audits of home schooling environments and ongoing achievement testing of the children.
- This Platform also suggests revamping curricula.
  - o There is an overwhelming amount of research to support that children have different proclivities at different stages (*i.e.*, the ability to learn languages, develop math skills, etc.). Elementary, middle, and high school curricula should be adjusted to reflect this.
  - o All courses that have been introduced to allow us to feel more *"progressive"* and *"politically correct"* shall immediately be repositioned or eliminated. I've done an informal survey, and most First Graders really don't indicate a need to learn about birth control. It turns out, when they ask the inevitable question, *"Mommy and Daddy, where did I come from?"* ... they're usually looking for an answer like Cincinnati or Dallas.

- In concert with *real* **Health Care Reform, physical education programs (both during and after school) will be reinstated.**
- **Similarly, school lunches will be monitored for quality and balance, and the students will be taught at an early age how to make healthier decisions.**
- **Correspondingly, students will be taught basic life skills to help them make better** *all-around* **decisions. For example:**

- **They will be taught how to read labels, compare ingredients, and to do the math to determine which packaging of a product offers the best value.**
- **They will be taught how to balance a check book.**
- **They will be taught when credit is good ... and when it is not.**
- **They will be taught the essentials of** *"logic"* **to help them break complex issues into smaller, understandable components so they can learn how to question statements, ads, and political promises to determine what's true ... and what's not.**

Essentially, students will be taught how to make *intelligent, informed* decisions. Not *every* child goes to college ... nor *should* they; but *every* child should be *prepared* to *pursue happiness*, and *every* child should be *intellectually insulated* from being *misled* by gimmicks, verbal misrepresentations, or *"slick"* marketing hype. Otherwise, they will be condemned to suffer the same poor choices of the current generations (college age and older), including our choice of political representation. There's *got* to be a better answer!

By reforming this Nation's K-12 educational system, we will automatically improve our university system as well. Much like this Platform's call for more qualified political candidates, the reformation of our K-12 educational system will provide candidates to our colleges and universities who are better prepared. In the interim, this Platform calls for the redirection of the billions of tax dollars that are currently doled out to public and private universities. We should be investing in our greatest asset: our leaders of tomorrow. In that regard:

- We should *eliminate* all of the ridiculous qualifications that are tied to academic funding that emanates from the Federal government; qualifications that are in place principally to allow the government to exert more pressure on academic institutes to conform to the government's view of what education should be (including the imposition of quotas, the management of social folkways, etc.).
- If the Federal government is going to make an investment in *each* student, then it should parallel the *"voucher"* approach that was previously described.
  - *Students* should be allowed to decide whether they wish to attend a public or private university, and the stipend could be so directed. It is up to the colleges and universities to remain *"competitive"* with regard to the education and experience they deliver.
  - If the Federal government *really* wants to make a difference, it should create a tiered structure to address *"educational investment;"* not unlike the concept behind a progressive tax ... except that this one makes *sense*.
- A modest stipend could be provided as to acknowledge the of accomplishment to *all* students who *qualify* for and *elect* to attend a college or university;
- A more significant stipend could be awarded to those students who achieved *above average* performance throughout their high-school careers; and
- A *"full ride"* could be offered to students whose academic performance in high school was truly *exceptional*.
  - This would provide an incentive to *all* students to perform to the best of their abilities in high school. It's Affirmative Action at its finest: it *affirms* that *if* students take the *actions* that are necessary to earn *good* to *great* grades in high school, they will be assisted with their college education *regardless* of their race, religion, gender, and sexual-orientation ... or whether they happen to be great athletes. *Every* student will have an *equal* opportunity to excel and, in effect, to shape the future of their lives. Even young adults from rich families would have the opportunity to *earn* something on their own;

not because of having won the DNA lottery ... but because *they* worked hard to establish their *own* success.

Who knows? Over time, *"We the People ..."* might even become a more meaningful phrase to our future leaders if they are allowed to truly experience the feeling of having been *created equal* with the *unalienable right* to *pursue happiness*. And rather than bury our future generations in unwarranted debt born out of imprudent government, let's allow them to bask in freedom and educate them in a way that guarantees their ability to do the same for every generation that follows.

Educational reform effectively requires generational change ... and it might take *two* generations to get us back to where the Framers had hoped we would be. Despite what we have done to ourselves, we remain the *greatest Nation on Earth*. The fact that we have an immigration problem is evidence of that fact. I rather doubt that Afghanistan needs much of a fence to protect its borders from illegal immigration. Somehow, I think its suppression of human rights is enough to curb the flow. People come here for a reason: the United States of America offers them the greatest *opportunity* to achieve *personal* success. Those who immigrate to our country, legally or illegally, are looking for the chance to take advantage of that opportunity. If we want to stem the tide of illegal immigration without having to enforce our laws, all we have to do is to *stop* defending our citizens' *Lives* and *Liberties* and to deny their *pursuit of Happiness*. We *cannot* afford to let that happen.

So ends the *National Platform of Common Sense*.

EPILOGUE

Thomas Jefferson was an incredibly talented individual and our Nation's *political* equivalent to Leonardo DaVinci when it comes to the depth and breadth of his intellect. Jefferson wrote our *Declaration of Independence*, contributed to the development of our *Constitution* and *Bill of Rights*, served as our *first* Secretary of State, *second* Vice President, and *third* President. In my opinion, he was a man of <u>uncommon</u> common sense. I leave you with a few of his quotes as a gift to inspire your thoughtful reflection with respect to what this country has been, what it is today, and what it can be moving forward. Though each of us may view this work of art called the United States of America and see something different, Thomas Jefferson gives us great insight into the very fabric of its soul.

    May you enjoy your *Life* … your *Liberty* … and the opportunity to pursue your every *Happiness*.

    May God Bless You, and May God Bless America.

"I would rather be exposed to the inconveniences attending too much liberty than to those attending too small a degree of it."

"The two enemies of the people are criminals and government, so let us tie the second down with the chains of the Constitution so the second will not become the legalized version of the first."

"Power is not alluring to pure minds."

"Experience hath shewn, that even under the best forms [of government] those entrusted with power have, in time, and by slow operations, perverted it into tyranny."

"I am not a friend to a very energetic government. It is always oppressive."

"Most bad government has grown out of too much government."

"The course of history shows that as a government grows, liberty decreases."

"Government big enough to supply everything you need is big enough to take everything you have."

"I think myself that we have more machinery of government than is necessary, too many parasites living on the labor of the industrious."

"The Republic will cease to exist when you take away from those who are willing to work and give to those who would not."

"I am persuaded that the good sense of the people will always be found to be the best army. They may be led astray for a moment, but will soon correct themselves. The people are the only censors of their governors, and even their errors will tend to keep these to the true principles of their institution. To punish these errors too severely would be to suppress the only safeguard of the public liberty."

Thomas Jefferson
April 13, 1743 – July 4, 1826

www.ingramcontent.com/pod-product-compliance
Lightning Source LLC
Chambersburg PA
CBHW032115090426
42743CB00007B/363